Head
in the
Sand

...and other unpopular positions

Other Books by Linda M. Au

Humor:

Fork in the Road . . . and other pointless discussions
Train of Thought: Travel Essays from a One-Track Mind
Travel Documents

Novels:

Secret Agent Manny
The Scarlet Letter Opener (Red Ink Mystery #1)
The Tell-Tale Heart Attack (Red Ink Mystery #2)
Charlotte's Website (Red Ink Mystery #3)
Gray Area

Head in the Sand

...and other unpopular positions

Linda M. Au

with a foreword by Patricia Lorenz

ISBN: 978-1-954973-03-9

Visit Linda online:
lindaau.com

Follow Linda on Twitter:
@LindaMAu

Stalk Linda on Facebook:
facebook.com/AuthorLindaMAu/

Cover art by Mike Ferrin (www.mikeferrin.org)

Vicious Circle Publishing
www.viciouscirclepublishing.com
viciouscirclepublishing@gmail.com

For Wayne . . .
who allows me to cannibalize my life with him
without even smiling

and

For the rest of my family and friends
(who shall remain nameless, except that I wrote about
them and didn't change their names) . . .
who tolerate my inappropriate people-watching
and note-taking at family gatherings

Ehh, forget about that "remain nameless" thing . . .
This includes, but is not limited to:
Mom & Dad
Mike & Cindy
Christopher & Courtney
Jeremy
Grace
Addie
Lynne
Fara
Mel
Mary Beth
Ginnie
Wayne's entire extended family
The Deep Creek Four (Sarah, Jeannine, Chris & me)
First Word and St. Davids
CritClub, especially ChopOMatic & Myriam
Easton Area High School (circa late-1970s)
The entire RPCNA
The Warpies writers
The gang at Movie Forums
The AlphaSmart group on Flickr
Café Kolache, where many of these essays were written

Contents

And the Award Goes to . . .

A tidy handful of the essays in this book have already ventured out into the world. Many have been criticized . . . I mean, *critiqued* . . . by my writers' group, First Word, which meets monthly in Sewickley, Pennsylvania. They gave me the self-esteem I needed to start entering essays in contests around the country. I am grateful to them for helping me nitpick my work over the past few years and laughing at stuff in all the right places (and some of the wrong ones).

Some essays have gone even further, winning awards in those contests, a few of which actually included money. No, seriously.

And so, since these early accolades led me to believe I could actually write, here's a list of awards garnered by some of the essays in this book:

"Dear Santa . . ." won **First Place** in Humor at the St. Davids Christian Writers' Conference, 2005.

"Rash Behavior" won **First Place** in Humor at the St. Davids Christian Writers' Conference, 2003.

"Tightening Your Belt" won **Second Place** in Humor at the St. Davids Christian Writers' Conference, 2004.

"Brave New World . . . Scared Old Mom" won **First Place** (and a big fat check that didn't bounce) in Humor & Technology at BrassRing's launch contest, 2000.

"Everything You Always Wanted to Know About Cement, But Were Afraid to Ask" won **First Place** in Humor at the St. Davids Christian Writers' Conference, 2006.

"Pennies in the Couch" won **Second Place** in Personal Experience Feature at the St. Davids Christian Writers' Conference, 2005.

"Say Ahhh!" won **First Place** in Life-Changing Moment at the Mercer One-Day Writers Conference, 2003.

"Household Chores" won **Third Place** in Humorous Poetry at the St. Davids Christian Writers' Conference, 2008.

"O Sing of Spring!" won **Second Place** in Light Poetry at the Mercer One-Day Writers Conference, 2010.

"Hell on Wheels" won **Honorable Mention** in Childhood Memory at the Mercer One-Day Writers Conference, 2007.

Foreword

Linda Au is the funniest woman I've ever met. In 2006 and 2007 I was asked to teach a few classes at the St. Davids Writers' Conference in Pennsylvania and Linda was one of the conference participants. The one who left the biggest impression. We instructors awarded Linda a number of well-deserved prizes for her entries in the writers' contests that week and of course I smiled and acted all proud of her, but inside I felt the green monster of envy building up. Mostly I envied her ability to write humor. . . . Okay, I became insanely jealous of her enormous talent. Then I decided if you can't beat 'em, join 'em, so I embarked on a quest to get her to either travel with me so her hilarious personality could rub off on me a little . . . or move to Florida where I live so I could pick her brain and spend my last forty to fifty years on earth being a better, funnier writer myself because of her.

I dreamed of having Linda Au as my sidekick, sailing with me through life, getting into all sorts of trouble, having adventures, exploring the world and yes, both of us writing funny, funny stuff which we could critique for each other in coffee shops drinking tea and howling uproariously. I suggested a writers-only cruise with some of our favorite writer friends. What I was thinking was, Hey, maybe if she spends a week with me on the open seas that'll convince her to uproot her family and move to Florida where we could be writing buddies forever, BFFs with a writing clause.

So far none of my grand schemes have worked. We haven't gone on a cruise together, traveled together, nor has she moved to Florida. Having come close to being selected to be on *Survivor* one year, she did convince me to also apply to be a contestant. How did she know I'd been dreaming of being on that show since season one? See what I mean about how much Linda and I have in common? So I applied in my 64th year because she told me they were looking for older women. That too, never came to be. They probably looked at my video and decided I was better off watching the sunsets on the beach than digging for oysters with my bare hands and living on coconut juice.

Meanwhile, I have gone on to write a few more books and Linda continues to tell me that she's definitely planning to retire to Florida someday partly because her husband has close family in this section of paradise. I'll believe it when I get the phone call: "Hey, meet me at the coffee shop and bring your laptop. I have some great ideas for a book we can do together."

All I can say about this woman author is this: She's funnier than me. She's younger than me. She's a better writer than me. She's smarter than me. Her best quirk is that she is a spelling-grammar-copy-editor-proof-reader genius, having made her living for awhile as an editor and she's going to pitch a holy fit when she reads the four sentences in front of this one because she'll say it should be "She's funnier than I." But I think it sounds better with "me." And since she asked me to write this foreword to her book, I get to say whatever I want and she can't change it. At least I think that's the way it works. I'm doubled over right now slapping my thighs. Which are bigger than hers, by the way.

I love this book. This funny, funny book. (Note the incomplete sentence, Linda?) Every story is funny. The way Linda Au looks at life should be bottled and sold as a panacea for eternal youth. I bet she never gets ulcers because of her funny, irreverent outlook on every single event in her life, big or small. She makes things like her husband's tool chest and his TV-watching habits funny as all get-out. You need a tissue when you read this book to mop up the laughing tears. She makes teaching her mom how to use a computer, the art of folding sheets, a letter to Santa, renewing her wedding vows in Vegas, a head cold, a water bed, a wedding ring, soap operas, roller-skating, people-watching, bathrobes, fishing trips, and even lunch at the nuclear power plant the funniest things since whoopee cushions were placed on all the nursing home chairs. You're going to love this book and no doubt you'll be as jealous of Linda Au as I am. After you finish reading it, please write to Linda and tell her it's time she moved to Florida. ❖

Patricia Lorenz
Author of a dozen books,
including *Life's Too Short To Fold Your Underwear*

www.PatriciaLorenz.com

Introduction

Hi. Welcome to my book. Pull up a chair and stay a while. I like your hair like that. And I love those shoes. Okay, enough flattery. We're moving on now.

You don't have to be a wife or mother, as I am, to identify with the stuff in this book. You just have to know a wife or a mother. That's close enough.

I'd love to say that everything in this book is completely true . . . or that everything in this book is completely made up. Either way I'm going to be in a boatload of trouble with *somebody*. So, to keep from being lynched in the restroom of the local craft store, let me assert with unabashed honesty that everything in this book is as true as it needs to be in order to be funny. When starting each of these essays, my goal was to exaggerate when necessary to keep the humor up around belly-button level (because belly-buttons are funny).

Imagine my surprise to find out just how little I had to exaggerate once I really got rolling. These people I grew up with and hang out with and live with are just naturally funny. Well, from a slight distance, anyway. They just don't know it yet.

Still, I'll leave the specifics of exactly which parts are true and which merely further the cause of humor up to you, dear reader. Because nobody I've mentioned in this book is going to admit to anything. Not without a lot of coaxing and a cashier's check.

So, now that the legal garbage is out of the way, just who do I think I am writing this stuff? A little background: I was raised in the sixties and seventies by a mother who drove a Fiero in the eighties and listened to Pink Floyd and a father who drove a pickup truck and listened to Johnny Cash. Somehow, all that genetic material added up to me.

Me? I drive cars old enough to vote and listen to "Weird Al" Yankovic. I know, I know. It doesn't make sense to me, either.

But I take hope for the future of our family—because my kids drive nicer cars than I do . . . and listen to Pink Floyd and Johnny Cash.   ♣

Dear Santa . . .

Dear Santa,

I've tried to be a good wife and mommy this year. I've hardly ever cursed under my breath upon finding the toilet seat up . . . in the middle of the night . . . in the dark. I only cut off idiot drivers on the parkway once or twice . . . a week. And I almost never find myself saying things my own mommy used to say to me, like, "Your face is going to freeze that way," or "I'll give you something to cry about," or even, "If I hear that instant message sound *one more time*!" Okay, fair enough. My mommy never used to say that last one. But, she would have.

With my otherwise stellar behavior in mind, Santa, I offer you the following wish list for the next holiday season:

I want the secret of how to maintain a clean house without having to worry about things like wiping down the baseboards. Baseboards are a tool of the devil.

I want a vacuum cleaner with a remote control. One strong enough to pick up signals from, say, Hawaii.

I'm not impressed with a window cleaner that doesn't streak. I want windows that don't streak.

I want mothers to come with built-in recording systems to match our already uncanny knack for remembering conversations verbatim. Because no matter how many times I can quote to my teenager his promise to finish cleaning his room, unless I got it on tape, I got nothing.

I want to be the kind of person who doesn't panic when she hears one of her "tidy" friends say she has to get home to take down all her mini-blinds and soak and scrub them—"because it's spring." What is that supposed to mean? She has to be O.C.D., right? I take mine down only when the three-year-old gets a glob of bright blue Colgate tartar-control gel smeared on them low enough for someone of average height to see. If he smears white toothpaste on white mini-blinds, I figure I've got another few months before it calcifies. And, if he flicks it so high that only a basketball player can see it, I know I've just bought myself a good year and a half without having to think about it . . . unless Wilt Chamberlain stops by. In fact, I can probably group that mishap with another event to be named later and then decide that the two events combined warrant taking the blinds down.

I want a software program that will not only balance my checkbook but will deposit extra money into my account when I'm overdrawn.

I want some sort of written guarantee that, when I lose weight (okay, *if* I lose weight), it won't all come off my chest first and my gut last.

I want a cat that knows the difference between my leg and a scratching post.

I want a dog that knows the difference between my leg and . . . never mind.

I don't want a shampoo with the conditioner built right in. I want a shampoo with the hair stylist built right in. If I can't have that, then just let me use the shampoo and conditioner separately. Time in the bathroom is the only time I get alone these days, and I want it to last as long as possible.

Oh, and yeah, I almost forgot: I want world peace. And let it begin with my kids.

Thank you, Santa. I look forward to working with you again this year. ✤

Even Jesus Doesn't Save Everything

My husband, Wayne, saves everything. And I mean everything. He saves more than a Unitarian Jesus.

In my husband's pockets you'll find crumpled up old receipts from trips to McDonald's drive-thrus for a diet Coke. Just a diet Coke. No sandwich. No fries. No two-hot-apple-pies-for-a-dollar. Just the Coke. These receipts are so ancient and wrinkled that the purplish mimeo ink has faded or smeared so badly you can't read it. Not that you'd need to.

He saves envelopes from our bills. Well, you say, you need those envelopes to send the payments back. Well, I say, no we don't, because we pay all our bills online. Besides, I wasn't even talking about *those* envelopes. (And yes, before you ask, he saves those too.) I was talking about the envelopes the bills came to the house in. The ripped-open envelopes that now have absolutely no earthly use at all except to scribble down impromptu grocery lists. And no, he doesn't use them to scribble down impromptu grocery lists. He just saves them.

He saves catalogs. And not just to give himself something to read in the bathroom. I'm talking department store catalogs so old they're having sales on leisure suits and Earth shoes. (*"Hurry! Sale ends in 1972!"*)

He saves phone numbers and addresses. All of them. In his computer. In his cell phone. In his PDA. He syncs more often than a lead balloon. Well, you say, this is a good thing. You never know who you might need to call or send Christmas cards to. And, if that were all it was, I'd agree with you. But every Christmas I ask him for his half of the Christmas card list (the addresses and names of his friends and family), and I always get a handful of names on his printout with multiple possible addresses. Seems people move once in a while, or change phone numbers. And when they do, he doesn't just replace their old information with their new information. Nope. He *saves* the old phone numbers and addresses. Like, what? Are they going to change their minds and move back to the old house?

So, when we needed the phone number for a campground we visit, he dug three phone numbers out of his PDA—unsure which one (if any) was the right one. Naturally, the first one had long since been disconnected. The second one was an answering machine, but at least it was the right phone number. I'm still not sure what the third phone number was. Probably their *future* phone number.

He saves bent nails, plastic bags, old sneakers (and I don't mean just the previous pair he used to wear—I mean three and four generations earlier than the pair he wears currently), old underwear (can you say, "dust rag"?), old T-shirts with holes and pit stains (can you say, "big dust rag"?), old pairs of glasses (is he expecting his eyes to revert back to an earlier prescription?), old raffle ticket stubs (the contest is over, he didn't win, but he's taking the phrase "eternal optimist" to new heights), old physics textbooks from college (great bedtime reading, I guess), old AAA guide books filled with places that have long since closed or burned down, and anything else under the sun about which he can say, "You never know. I might need this later."

Which, as it turns out, is just about everything. It's a battle cry for the ages.

Does it bug me? Actually, I'm awfully glad he likes keeping all his old, useless, broken-down stuff . . . because that includes me.   ♣

Rash Behavior

I have an unexplained rash across my body. People talk in hushed tones around me. Dogs whimper and run for cover when I go outside.

It isn't poison ivy. I never get poison ivy, ever—even if I chew on the leaves and wash them down with a sumac chaser. This is an insidious, *crawling* thing, covering me like a creeping fungus.

After I give up on home diagnosis, I go to my new, young doctor. He scratches his hairless chin, peeks under my paper gown a little, says things like "Huh!" and "Gee!", and shakes his head.

"Can I call in an associate? I have *no clue* what this is."

We call in an associate.

Doctor #2 prods me a while. He looks twice the age of Doctor #1. He scratches his chin, peeks under my flimsy paper gown a little more, and says things like, "Wow!" and "You're right!" He shakes his head and asks, "Can we call in *another* doctor?"

Doctor #3 is added to our motley crew, and, judging from the dialogue, I've stepped right into a Marx Brothers movie.

The only thing they agree on is that I should see a dermatologist. Like, *yesterday*. One dermatologist offers me an appointment for next Thanksgiving. Did I mention how much I love my new HMO?

After my doctor's receptionist badgers another dermatologist into an appointment the same week, I feel the resolution can't be far behind. I return from that visit with the following information at my fingertips (which are the only parts of me left without the rash):

• *The good news* is that the dermatologist had to ask me only two simple questions before she made a diagnosis.
• *The bad news* is that I'll have to pay $125 for that five minutes if my new insurance hasn't kicked in yet.

• *The good news* is that the disorder has a name: *pityriasis rosea*.
• *The bad news* is that even that homeschooled Indian kid would have been stumped on this one in the National Spelling Bee.

- *The good news* is that it's not contagious.
- *The bad news* is that people don't believe you that it's not contagious.

- *The good news* is that it's like chicken pox: You get it only once and then develop a lifelong immunity.
- *The bad news* is that it's like chicken pox: It itches like crazy, spreads everywhere, and looks absolutely disgusting.

- *The good news* is that it will go away on its own.
- *The bad news* is that it will go away on its own because no one knows how it gets there in the first place. "It will go away on its own" is a doctor's catch-all phrase for ninety percent of the ailments I have ever had.

- *The good news* is that there is a progression this rash follows, and it looks normal for the three-week mark.
- *The bad news* is that it lasts eight to twelve weeks.

- *The good news* is that the dermatologist prescribed two steroid creams for the itching.
- *The bad news* is that one of them burns off three layers of skin, and the other one does about as much good as rubbing Crisco on my torso.

- *The good news* is that my pharmacy has a drive-thru window so I won't have to go inside with this ugly rash.

- *The bad news* is our new health plan isn't accepted at this pharmacy.

- *The good news* is there is another pharmacy with a drive-thru window only a few blocks away, and they take my health plan.
- *The bad news* is I have to walk in anyway because the plastic drive-thru vacuum tube I am supposed to put my prescription into slips out of my hands and rolls under my car, and I accidentally run over it.

- *The good news* is I slip past the front counter without anyone seeing me carrying fifty pieces of crushed plastic.
- *The bad news* is they are all staring at my rash instead, and the pharmacists in the back of the store probably wonder what other medications I am on to have demolished a big plastic tube at one mile per hour.

- *The good news* is that oatmeal baths relieve the itching enough to go to bed at night.
- *The bad news* is that my husband prefers Cream of Wheat.   ♣

Tightening Your Belt

I t is bad. Really bad. We rip up the old living room carpet and realize we have to sand down the shredded chunks of petrified wood underneath. My husband, though, is giddy with anticipation. As I wrestle the furniture out of the room, he runs to the basement and drags out his belt sander, ripping the ratty old belt off and slipping a new belt on with ease.

Then he reaches for the thingamajig that tightens the belt. It isn't there. None of the handles on the contraption tighten anything—except his forehead, which is pinched so tight I fear an aneurysm.

"Why don't I look in that drawer where you keep the owner's manuals for everything you've owned since sixth grade?" I offer.

"Somebody gave this to me secondhand. I never

had the manual." If there's anything Wayne loves more than a new tool, it's a *free* tool.

His first impulse is to do a Google search for "belt sander" to see if the manufacturer has a thousand-page schematic he can print out and stuff in a desk drawer until 2037. I remind him that we have just dismantled the computer and moved it out of the living room so we can rip up the carpet.

He mumbles things I've only heard on cable TV and sits down in the middle of the bare wooden floor, pondering the sander from every angle. I watch him from across the room, fascinated, the same way Jane Goodall watches chimps. Before he can start grooming me for lice, I suggest that he call my dad, who owns every power tool known to mankind and sorts them in his garage by size and function. (He's retired and has nothing better to do than fix things that aren't broken yet.)

Wayne ignores me and taps the sander with a ball peen hammer. *Tap. Tap. Tap.* I admire his manly way of taking charge. He grunts, then snorts. Then grunts again. I admire him some more.

I cross the room to the phone and call my dad, asking him if he owns a similar belt sander. Naturally, he does. Wayne sits with his back to me, his derriere collecting jagged edges of floorboard with the same speed my daughter collects Barbie shoes. I say loudly and not-at-all subtly, "Dad, *he's right here*," and then hand Wayne the phone. It is a short conversation.

"Uh-huh . . . . Ohhhhh."

Wayne grabs a screwdriver, winds up, and whacks the side of the sander, which makes a small clicking noise.

"Huh. You're right. It worked."

Another home repair problem solved. And no head lice. Jane Goodall would be so proud. ♣

Brave New World . . . Scared Old Mom

Technology turned our mother-daughter relationship upside down. Without being asked, I had become the mommy of my mommy. I was the one in charge, teaching her so that she might one day toddle out on her own and forge her way in the Brave New World.

The Brave New World, that is, of cyberspace.

It started innocently enough back in the mid-nineties. While most older folks were moving to Florida, my parents retired at age fifty-five and moved two thousand miles away to Las Vegas. It was drier and warmer than Pennsylvania, they said. It was dirt cheap to live there, they said. It was their one big adventure in life, they said. This'll never work, I said.

My brother and I bit our lips and let them go with a kiss and a prayer—and a roll of nickels.

It soon became obvious that the distance was going to be more daunting than anyone had anticipated. Despite the technology of the telephone, contact became more sporadic because it was costly—and because of the time difference. They now lived in a world of early rising, 110-degree "it's-a-dry-heat," and four P.M. cheap buffets on the Strip. By the time the phone rates dropped at the end of their day, they themselves had dropped hours earlier, snoozing during *Murder, She Wrote.*

I've been online since 1988 and I know the value of quick, cheap communication such as e-mail. One day in the mid-nineties, I casually mentioned to a friend that it would be nice to get a cheap, secondhand computer for my parents so they could get online and keep in touch better. Soon I was offered a free low-end 286 computer and monitor. [*Author's Note:* There's no such thing as a free lunch—or a free computer.] With a little tweaking, my parents could use it to get started.

Several hundred dollars later, I was belatedly rethinking my strategy.

My mother seemed more eager than my dad to venture into this new technology. She had, after all, used customized computer programs in her job as a quality control technician for the Crayola crayon company for years. (My father's expertise in high technology had been limited to hot-wiring and souping up the VCR—apparently so that it would flash "1:00" instead of "12:00.")

I timed the arrival of the upgraded computer at their house to coincide with my visit to them that spring. I arrived on Tuesday, and the second-day air packages arrived on Wednesday. I hooked everything up effortlessly and we were on our way. That week I gave my mom the perfunctory training she'd need to maneuver around Windows and AOL, and I left Las Vegas confident that we'd soon be e-mailing and sending instant messages to each other on a regular basis. After all, how hard was AOL to figure out?

I swear on the grave of my Tandy 2000 that I had no sooner stepped in my door and dropped my duffel bag than the phone rang.

"Hello?"

"Linda? Hi! You're home? How was your flight?"

"Fine, Mom. I just got home. What's up? Is everything all right?"

"Everything's fine. I just have one teeeeensy question, though."

Her emphasis on the word "teeeeensy" didn't go unnoticed.

"Go ahead, shoot."

"It's about the computer."

I felt a slight tightening in my throat, but dismissed it as jet lag. *Everything is fine.... Everything is fine.*

I sat down.

"Yes?"

"It won't turn on."

The tightening became a lump. *Never buy a used computer*, I thought.

"What do you mean, it won't turn on?"

"I push in the button like you showed me, and nothing happens."

The lump began to pulse rhythmically. Maybe my dad had hot-wired it. *Abandon hope, all ye who enter here,* I thought fleetingly.

"What do you mean, nothing happens?"

"I mean, nothing happens. Zilch. Nothing."

"What about the switch on the monitor?"

"Nope. Nothing there either. Weird, huh?"

"Mom . . . Did you turn on the power strip first?"

"What's a power strip?"

One problem down. Thirty-seven thousand to go.

I think I had time to unpack and eat a meal or two before the next phone call came in.

"Hi, honey. I hate to bother you, but. . . . It's the computer again."

"Doesn't it turn on?"

"Oh, it's on. That's not it."

I felt strangely relieved. She was teachable, at least.

"Then what's the problem?" I asked.

"The thingy is blinking."

"The what is what?"

"The thingy is blinking."

"Mom, you'll have to speak up. It sounds like you're saying, 'The thingy is blinking.'"

"It IS blinking!" she insisted. "And I keep hearing this crunching noise."

Twenty minutes and an entire lack of jargon later, I ascertained that the "thingy" in question was the hard disk activity light on the CPU. The crunching noise was, of course, the hard disk activity indicated by the blinking thingy.

My mother began to get the hang of being online quickly after that. Soon she could forward joke e-mails to several hundred of her closest friends and type "LOL ;-) " in an instant message window with the best of them. Suddenly I had more daily contact with my mother than I'd had in the womb. Despite the cyber-claustrophobia, it was nice to have her feel close again.

Several months went by. Little questions trickled in now and then.

1. "I swear I was just gone from the computer for ten minutes, and I came back and there were these swirling colored lines dancing all over the screen. Where did everything go?"

2. "I saved this letter to your brother, and now I can't find it. I think the computer hid it from me."

3. "I got the picture of the kids you sent me with your e-mail, but I don't know how to open it again to show your father."

4. "Okay, I found the picture but when I opened it this time it took up the whole screen."

5. "I tried to install something, but it wouldn't let me. . . . What? Honestly, I don't know. It just kept telling me no."

6. "I know this was a used computer, honey, but I

just found some old folder on here from the previous owner, called 'Teen JPGs.' Don't tell your father. He'd die."

After a lot of trial and error, my mother learned to write down for me exactly what happened when an error occurred. She now wrote down the information in the little dialog box with the red "X" before clicking on "OK." We began to solve her problems on the first try. And I began to wonder if I'd missed my calling as a tech support rep.

Other than basic computer training, things went smoothly. And together, we got that computer tweaked and humming, and kept her and my dad in touch with the big, wide world. Then one day I got another call from my mother.

"Hi, Lindy Lou. . . . How are ya, honey?"

She'd called me Lindy Lou. She was priming me for something. Something big.

"Hi, Mom. What's up?"

She sighed. "Ohhh. . . . It's the computer. It broke."

"What do you mean, 'it broke'?"

"The guy at the shop said the hard drive died. He said this happens sometimes when hard drives get older, and it's probably for the best."

She sounded as if an old maiden aunt had died. And was that sniffling I heard on the other end of the phone?

"Mom, I'm sorry. I probably should have saved up more and gotten you a better computer."

"No, it's okay. I feel bad since you spent all that time on it. The good news is that your father and I traded it in for a brand-new computer with everything on it!"

I could tell how proud and excited she was. She always said "your father and I" for the big stuff.

This new-fangled contraption had Windows 98—and I was still lumping along with Windows 95. It had enough bells and whistles to rival all the slots on the Strip. She gushed on the phone that it did disk cleanup automatically at one o'clock in the morning, and that it defragmented her hard drive when she was shopping—things I'd only read about. I tried hard not to get my knickers in a twist.

Every day I got a dozen e-mails from my mom: spam about Madalyn Murray O'Hara; forwarded jokes with more ">>>'s" in every line than actual text; URL links to online newspaper articles about diseases she was afraid I'd get; and recipes I'd never use because I don't routinely keep goat cheese or spices from as-yet undiscovered countries in my kitchen.

Despite all the warm, homey contact online, my life felt strangely hollow. It wasn't until months later that I realized what was missing: those unexpected phone calls from my technologically-challenged mother. She hadn't had a problem with her computer in months. On her own, she e-mailed her senator every week, IMed with her grandchildren, played ten different variations of Solitaire, designed flyers for the neighborhood casino-zoning meetings at their house, and successfully installed videocam software.

It was obvious, even to me, that she was ready. And, much to my relief, the Brave New World welcomed her with open arms.   ♣

The Rule of Law in Florida

Little-known laws I discovered while
visiting the Sunshine State in 2000

Celebrating Christmas in southwestern Florida during a historic election year was certainly unique. Between ballot recounts while watching in horror everyone's hanging chads, I had enough time on my hands to compile a list of rules for living there. It took my mind off the election brouhaha.

RULE: At Christmas, you must over-decorate your house with icicle lights, even though you haven't seen an icicle since you got that frost-free refrigerator in 1986.
REASON: You must trick Santa into thinking it's cold enough to show up in that stifling red suit.

RULE: You must wear sweaters and hats if the temperature dips below 62 degrees.

REASON: This alerts the tourists that you're a local when a wind-chill factor of 58 sends shivers up your spine. This doesn't stop you from going to the beach, of course. You just wear mittens.

RULE: You must own a car the size of a 40-foot schooner.

REASON: Most Floridians own cars that can be mistaken for small yachts in the parking lot of the Winn-Dixie. This is to protect them from the rare but elusive soccer mom wielding a dangerous SUV without using her left turn signal.

RULE: You cannot have a basement.

REASON: All building contractors in Florida are afraid of ancient burial grounds. But where do you put the broken bicycles, chest freezers, and power tools?

RULE: You must own a two-car attached garage with as much square footage as your house, even if you own only one car.

REASON: You'll need room for your broken bicycles, chest freezers, and power tools. The rest of the garage is used to dock your car.

RULE: If you're a tourist, you must always wear shorts, Birkenstock knock-offs, and T-shirts everywhere you go.

REASON: Even though it's 40 degrees at night, friends back home are being tortured by snowdrifts, so you're determined to get pictures of yourself near the ocean in shorts, Birkenstock knock-offs, and a T-shirt.

RULE: The only roadkill your tourist friends will ever see this far south is a dead armadillo.

REASON: The alligators eat all the other wildlife.

RULE: When taking walks, you're permitted to experience a small hill, but only if you're on a golf course.

REASON: Florida is really just Kansas with a lot more water. And fewer tornadoes. But more hurricanes.   ♣

Three Sheets to the Wind

I just finished folding bedsheets fresh from the dryer. There is a knack to folding elasticized, fitted queen-sized sheets so they'll lay flat in a drawer and take up less space (and get less wrinkled till you use them). My mother taught me how to do this when I was a young girl—patiently (or not so patiently, depending on my perspective at age ten or age forty-nine) and with a precision that I can still duplicate in just a minute or two to this very day. I can do it properly even with my eyes closed. It scares me a little.

It's one of those housekeeping skills I shied away from learning as a girl but can now appreciate as a middle-aged adult. It's beyond my own limited comprehension of physics to understand why the same sheet takes up far more space in the linen closet if I just give up and stuff it in there balled up in frustration rather than carefully folding it and placing it flat on the shelf alongside its peers. Isn't it the same sheet with the same square footage, the same amount of molecules? So why does it take up more space if I don't fold it first? I have always striven against menial chores that take up more brain space than they should, but in my house, the closet space is more limited than my brain space (and that's saying something). So, I grudgingly (but efficiently) fold the sheets and put them away. And, they fit.

Let me be clear, though: This is a skill that came from my mother. On my own, I would never have thought to neatly fold square pieces of cloth with cinched elastic that go onto a piece of furniture that's used in a private room of my house while I am essentially unconscious—pieces of cloth that are always hidden under *other* pieces of cloth that I spread over the sheets every morning precisely to cover them up. There is no logic to such a folding exercise, and I'd never have thought it up on my own, the physics of my small closets notwithstanding.

Of all the things I could have inherited from my Type-A personality mother, God chose the ability to both fold sheets properly and to wash dishes by hand within an inch of their lives. (I get my hair and eye color from my dad's side of the family, in case you were wondering.) My mother also squeegees her shower every time someone breathes on it, removes pieces of trash from the bathroom trash can throughout the day so that it's always empty, and hates her kitchen floor because it has microscopic grooves in the tiles where two or three atoms of dirt taunt her on Mondays, Wednesdays, and Fridays when she scrubs the floor with industrial-strength chemicals that require a gas mask and could eat the skin off an elephant in five seconds flat.

This is the woman who raised me. Honestly, I didn't stand a chance.

This may be my heritage—this may be the mother from whence I came—but it is not the mother I have become. But I wouldn't call it rebellion to say that I can look at a dirty baseboard in fascination for months before it begins to bother me—and even then it's usually because my mother is stopping by, and even *then* it's not enough for me to actually do anything about it. Not rebellion, really. More like confusion with a dash of inertia thrown in.

If I hadn't seen with my own eyes the birth certificate with both our names on it and the hospital photos and heard the stories of the million-hour labor, I'm not sure I'd believe she and I share the same DNA. Can all the genes from one's mother be 100% recessive? Because that would explain a lot.

Then again, I'm looking at those folded bedsheets right now, and they look damn good. There might be something to this science stuff after all.   ♣

What Happened in Vegas

A Diary: Part One

October 11, 2000

We're here in sunny Las Vegas—my husband, Wayne, nine-year-old Grace, and me—with blue skies overhead, the soft, gentle *ping-pinging* of slot machines everywhere (even in the Laundromats and Walmarts), and of course, the rough *rumble-rumble* of backhoes digging up my parents' entire street, down a foot and a half into the ground. In fact, the road we came in on from our hotel this morning is now closed this afternoon, and when we came back from our buffet lunch (see below), my parents' driveway was closed. No wonder my mom says the state bird of Nevada is the "crane."

The two flights in (for those of you who are still snickering at my panicky fear of flying) were as uneventful as I could have asked for. And trust me, I asked. The first leg (Pittsburgh to Charlotte, North Carolina) was over before Gracie could really get into it, although I personally could have done without her gawking out the window and gasping, "Wow, you should see how much the plane is *tilted*, Mom! I bet if I had my Coke here now, it'd spill out of the cup! Cool!" (Yeah, yeah, that's nice, Gracie, now here's a pillow. It's fun to *sleep* on a plane too.)

The second leg, to Las Vegas, was 4.75 hours long (or should I say, 4.75 *long hours*?), but not bad ("not bad" being a relative term). Reading several books and magazines helped, as did my portable CD player with Santana cranked up loud. (**Factoid of the Day:** Did you know that it is impossible to turn up a personal CD player loud enough to drown out engine noise without going clinically deaf?)

We were served dinner on this leg: a rather mediocre roast beef-type substance with something akin to rice and corn, an adorably teeny saladette, some dark brown, square thing that I think was a brownie at one time, a slice of cheese, crackers, and a dinner roll with Land O'Lakes butter. (Remind me to tell you Wayne's story of the legend of the Land O'Lakes girl. On second thought, don't.)

My enthusiasm for this meal was surpassed only by Gracie's, who eagerly commented on everything on her tray as if she'd never had such a sumptuous feast in her life. ("Look, Mom, a salad! Wow, crackers!" If only she were this easy to please at home.) When we caught her eating her brownie with her spoon after the meal, we asked why she hadn't just used her fork instead. She replied, "I just want to use *everything!*"

The only downer so far has been that Wayne spent the morning we left Pittsburgh in the local hospital instead of at work for half a day. Why? Seems he's developed some sort of odd infected bursitis in his right elbow, which had swollen up and been very uncomfortable. So, he's currently sitting in my dad's recliner across the room from me, doped up on several types of medication, suffering from jet lag, and aching from having had to squeeze his 6'4" frame into a 2'x2' plane seat for 4.75 long hours. (You do the math. You'll need a calculator. And yes, you can use scrap paper.) Good thing he looks cute with his knees up around his chin.

Picture this: We gave him the aisle seat, thinking that he could then prop his sore elbow up on a pillow hanging out into the aisle.

Rethink this: Don't try this if you are sitting at the back of the plane right around the only two restrooms on board. Before we lost count, his elbow had been bumped, jammed and poked forty-seven times per hour (all time zones included) by folks sprinting down the aisle toward the stalls.

Gracie is staying with my parents in their spare room. Well, actually it's their cat's room. Yes, their cat (named Joker—how appropriate for a cat in Las Vegas) has his own room. He has a daybed (complete with trundle) for when he has guest kitties over, a closet and drawers to keep all his stuff in, a clothes hamper (unsure what this is for), a Health Rider exercise machine (apparently he's afraid of developing love handles), a phone jack (for when he gets his own laptop and wants to get online), and a litter box.

Anyway, Gracie said when she moved her hands in the night, the cat jumped her and attacked her fingers. It seems he's tickled pink that Grandma and Pappy have given him his own personal cat-toy to keep in his room.

Today we toured Caesar's Palace, which has a huge FAO Schwarz store complete with a three-story moving Trojan Horse (everything has that Greco-Roman theme in Caesar's Palace, including the Warnerius Fraternius Storius, a.k.a. the Warner Brothers Store). You can go inside the belly of the horse itself, where you can be lured into buying all sorts of overpriced Trojan Horse keychains and hats, plus a one-of-three-in-the-world Trojan rocking horse for your child, as long as you have $12,500 you don't know what to do with. Yes, you read that right: four times what I paid for my used Corsica last year.

Caesar's Palace has an hourly show at the fountains, involving animatronic robots reenacting the fall of Atlantis, complete with actual fire storms, ice storms, and a gargoyle who signals the fall of Atlantis at Zeus' bidding. (Zeus is really just a hologram video on the domed ceiling, but don't tell the animatronic statues. It'll be our secret.)

We finished the day with a late-lunch buffet at Boulder Station Casino. (No one over fifty eats dinner after three P.M. here. It's against the law.) None of us will be hungry again until November.

The weather today has turned out to be about five degrees cooler than it is in Pittsburgh. My mother insists we brought the weather with us. I think anyone who owns an outdoor Jacuzzi in a gazebo and can wear shorts and a tank top on Christmas has no right to complain.

Since I have a husband tagging along on this trip for the first time, and my parents have a small house, Wayne and I are staying in a hotel a few miles away. We also have a rental car, which means I've now driven the Las Vegas Strip myself and lived to tell about it. It's not for the faint of heart, because sixty percent of the vehicles on the eight-lane road are taxicab minivans sporting huge signs of scantily-clad showgirls (which is why I don't want to let Wayne drive, lest he inadvertently become distracted and crash the car into the MGM Grand).

The rest of the day will be spent visiting my folks, lounging around their house, taking over their computer, annoying their cat, eating their food, and changing the channels on their TV when they leave the room for a minute. Life is good.

Upcoming events for the week include: Hoover Dam (otherwise known as "That Dam Tour"), the Treasure Island pirate battle, the Mirage volcano, the Excalibur casino where we will get a caricature done for Gracie (which I also had done for her brothers when they accompanied me here), and—late in the evenings when we leave Gracie here with my folks and head back to the hotel in the rental car—more quiet, peaceful time alone than Wayne and I have had in a long time.

Well, in a town like Las Vegas, in a hotel that doubles as a casino 24/7, I suppose saying "quiet, peaceful time alone" is really a relative term. But sometimes, being "alone" with hundreds of strangers banging on slot machines and collecting clanking quarters in metal containers can be quieter than time at home with six kids.

But, that's another adventure . . .

See you all later with more updates. And don't forget the big surprise for Wayne: Oct. 17, 2:30 Pacific Time . . . when we renew our wedding vows with Elvis himself live on the Web!

Continued on page 65 . . .

Everything You Always Wanted to Know About Cement

But Were Afraid to Ask

My husband is sitting here in the living room in his own personal Electronic Geek Heaven: He's become one with the La-Z-Boy recliner, feet up, new laptop on his, well, *lap* while it whirrs and hot-syncs to his teeny tiny PDA, the television remote control just inches away from his quivering right hand.

His eyes are focused on some generic show on the History Channel, or the Discovery Channel, or possibly the Learning Channel. Frankly, I can't tell them apart anymore now that they've melded into pretty much the same channel. They all air the same shows but with different titles.

On any given night, after I say the four stupidest words in the history of womankind ("Watch whatever you want"), I find myself knee-deep in either an hour-long documentary on the history of concrete, or a biker-building series where a bunch of men with greasy T-shirts and handlebar mustaches reconstruct motorcycles out of old Budweiser cans and toilet seats from outhouses they patronize somewhere on the outskirts of town.

I can hear that nasal twang emanating from the television even now . . . .

"Well, golly, we're behind schedule on Joe-Bob's commode-o-cycle, and we'll have to take shortcuts in order to get it done in time for the big contest in three days. So, I'm a-weldin' the seat lid to the carburetor and hopin' for the best. Meanwhile, Billy-John has gone and run a nail gun up through his nose . . . *again* . . . and we'll have to lose another two hours taking him to the Urgi-Care in Buckland County to have his sideburns sewed back on straight."

Now, I ask you: How many times do I want to watch the series *Modern Marvels* broadcast a show on why a suspension bridge works without everyone falling off, or a two-hour special on the story of a submarine that got lost at sea and killed everyone on board when one tiny part busted off, all because no one had bothered to watch the show on the history of concrete? What kind of man watches a show called *Major Engineering Disasters*? On purpose, I mean. What kind of woman **marries** such a man? On purpose, I mean.

Those were rhetorical questions. Do not answer them. There are no correct answers.

I admit that my husband and I both have somewhat

plebeian tastes when it comes to watching television. Like any decent Pittsburgh blue-collar male, I too enjoy a good Steelers game, a filthy grub-eating contest on *Survivor*, and even the occasional mobster series on HBO. My husband loves these shows even more than I do, but he always comes back to those "build-something-from-aluminum-foil-and-toothpicks" shows. It's only a matter of time before he starts taking notes during one of those foil-and-toothpick shows. I swear, if he ever leaves the confines of that La-Z-Boy and heads off to Home Depot while mumbling something about remodeling the bathroom with Reynold's Wrap, I'm outta here.

And I'm taking the remote control with me.

Oh no . . . I just remembered that we have ten spare universal remotes in a drawer of the coffee table, all programmed to work with the TV in case the other nine break at the same time.

Curses. Foiled again. ♣

Buster's Last Stand

The generation gap stops here. I'm cashing in on the video game craze with a game my kids can master with skills they already have. They grew up blowing into Nintendo game cartridges to get them to work, so this stuff is second nature to them. And since they're already experts, they'll enjoy mastering the game in record time. Here's my concept of how the game would play out on the screen:

LEVEL 1: *"Are These Your Shorts, Young Man?"*
Crazy, cute animal game character Buster tosses T-shirts, pants, and bunched-up boxers toward the hamper. If any laundry ends up *in* the hamper, deduct 10 points and game play moves to the laundry room. Level ends by climbing inside the dryer and locating the Missing Left Sock.

LEVEL 2: *"Your Eyes Will Freeze That Way"*

Buster makes goofy faces at dinner without being spotted by Mother. Ten points per face. Buster gets Bonus Star if Sister tattles on him and Mother doesn't believe her. Extra points if Sister hoists peas at him. Deduct points if peas hit Mother. Deduct 20 points if Buster is sent to his room without dinner. Add 20 points if he hates peas.

LEVEL 3: *"Isn't That Homework Done Yet?"*

Buster hides behind a stack of schoolbooks. Mother pops up intermittently outside the doorway, trying to catch Buster downloading MP3s instead of doing homework. Extra points for paper shuffling and pencil sharpening. Deduct 100 points if Buster completes any homework before dinner.

LEVEL 4: *"Were You Born In A Barn?"*

Buster avoids getting bopped in the backside by the screen door on his way in and out of the house. Five points for every insect that gets into the house, and 25 points for every slam that elicits a shriek from Mother. If she makes him go back out and come in quietly, he returns to the beginning of the level.

LEVEL 5: *"Take Out That Trash!"*

Buster stacks as much garbage as possible in the trash without actually taking it out. "Ctrl-G" picks up paper, banana peels, and spaghetti strands encrusted around old meatballs, and the spacebar drops it all on top of the heap. If it topples over and Mother makes him take out the trash, the game is over.

Why will kids play my game instead of *Sonic Mario Bandicoot Somethingorother*? Because I said so, young man. *And just wait until your father gets home!* ✤

What Happened in Vegas

A Diary: Part Two

October 12, 2000

Every Vegas update from me contains a food section. It's impossible to go to Las Vegas and not comment on the food. Well, maybe Calista Flockhart could pull it off, but certainly not me. (And that's all I have to say about that.)

Today's food experience was a place in northeast Las Vegas called Timber's. It's a burger joint. Doesn't sound very exciting yet, does it? What if I tell you that it has a burger called the Hoss Burger? Impressed yet? What if I tell you that the Hoss Burger is $8.95 and includes a huge basket of fries? Still not excited? Okay, how's this: The thing weighs 2½ to 3 pounds, sits on a huge bun, and takes up an entire nine-inch dinner plate. It's covered with cheese, lettuce, bacon, tomato, onion, ketchup, mayo—the works. They serve it on a huge plate, with a steak knife sticking up out of the middle of it. Apparently the knife is to perform crude emergency quadruple-bypass surgery once you finish eating the burger.

Normally, people buy the Hoss Burger and share it in groups. Everyone gets a smaller plate, and they use the knife to divide it up for everyone like an apple pie.

However . . .

There is this contest.
The Hoss Challenge.
It comes with four options.

OPTION 1: You (alone) finish an entire Hoss Burger. You get your name on their Hoss Burger Hall of Fame board.

OPTION 2: You finish two (yes, two) Hoss Burgers in an hour. You get both burgers free and your name on the Hall of Fame board.

OPTION 3: You finish two Hoss Burgers in half an hour. You get both free, your name on the board, and $100.

OPTION 4: You participate in their monthly contest to eat a Hoss Burger in the shortest amount of time. Prize is $100.

The bad news is that if you choose to participate in Options 2 or 3, you have to sit at a separate table from your dinner party and are scrutinized by the entire Timber's staff and probably the Nevada Gaming Commission.

My mom, Gracie, and I shared one Hoss Burger. I still don't feel well. Wayne wanted to try Option 2 or 3, but we didn't want him to sit somewhere else, so he chose the first option. He has now carved out his niche in this town! His name is on the Hall of Fame board! It took him 27 minutes to finish it, but he did it (after cutting it into quarters). He insisted he was just practicing and that he wants to go back tomorrow and try for Option 3. I insisted this is a stupid idea. I won.

For those of you wondering if Option 3 can be done, or how fast Option 4 has been done, here are the stats (which are listed on your placemat when you sit down):

Fastest Hoss Eater: Dan "The Hoss" Gordon, Age 29, 130 lbs.

Time? One Hoss Burger in 3 minutes 20 seconds
Two Hoss Burgers in 22 minutes
Three Hoss Burgers in 25 minutes, 34 seconds

If he ever ate a fourth Hoss Burger, it was probably on his way to the cardiac unit.

For those of you still perversely fascinated by this contest, here is the fine print that keeps the faint of heart (and arteries) away (and I quote):

• You must let your waitress know at the time of your order that you are taking the challenge.

• You must choose one challenge.

- You must complete both burgers, which are served at the same time.
- You must remain seated throughout the whole challenge. [*Author's Note:* Apparently there has been at least one binge-and-purge cheating incident.]
- You may not make any substitutions except for special sauce, catsup, or mayonnaise.
- You must clean your plate. No food can be left on your plate, in your hands, or mouth, or on the floor.
- All challenges are the complete Hoss Burger with cheese.

The only good news in this massive list of qualifiers is this one:

- Your fries are not a part of the challenge.

Well, that changes everything. You don't have to eat the basket of fries? Then sign me up.

I'm going into such detail about this because I found the entire experience oddly fascinating. The Hall of Fame board is actually now three boards filled with names. Some people put the dates they completed the challenge; some put their ages (the youngest I saw was fourteen—where were this kid's parents?). Among the hundreds of names, I spotted only two women's names.

I want to meet these women. I don't know why. I just do.

Tonight (after we pry Wayne out of the recliner with a small crane we'll borrow from the construction workers outside), we're going to roll him down the Strip to two nearby casinos.

Then we'll wheel Wayne back to the hotel on a flatbed truck and hoist him with his own petard into bed.

Later, I'll flip him over like a burger so he doesn't get bedsores. Excuse me while I go find a spatula.

Continued on page 75 . . .

The Good, the Bad, and the Plugly

When you're a woman who falls asleep in about 2.5 hours, it's interesting to be married to a man who falls asleep in about 2.5 *seconds*.

But it ceases to be interesting when that same man starts snoring in about 2.*6* seconds.

And, the snoring isn't your typical loud snorrrrrrre. Instead, my husband snores by breathing in, in a regular snore-noise. Then his exhale-snore sounds like he's puffing out a little puff of air: ***puh!*** It's kinda cute.

So, it's: zzzzzzzzzz ... [wait two seconds] ... *puh!*
zzzzzzzz ... [two seconds] ... *puh!*

So, every night I lie in the dark, hearing the first part (zzzzzzzzzz ...) and ... just ... waiting ... silently ... for the ... second ... part ... *where is it? where is it? wait for it ... one ... two ...* ***puh!***

Whew. I was beginning to wonder if he'd stopped breathing there for a minute. Yeah, that's real easy to fall asleep to. Not.

After trying to spend the rest of the night on the sofa (a colossally bad idea when you own an ancient sectional sofa with bumps where the sections meet), in an act of pure self-preservation I searched the shelves of Walmart and bought a bag of little green foam ear plugs. I was amazed to find they sell ear plugs at all. Turns out they even have them listed on the little overhead aisle marker sign:

Contact Lens Solution
Eyeglass Accessories
Ear Plugs

They're apparently *that* popular. After reading all the labels on all **ten** brands they sell, I now know more about ear plugs than any human being needs to know. Even in a capitalist society of competing brands, I assumed they'd have one set of little plastic cork-like things stashed in a corner somewhere. One size. One brand. No descriptions. Just, "Here are your ear plugs. They plug your ears. Now you can't hear. Now go away."

Instead, for a couple of bucks, I came home with ten pairs of green foamy stuff shaped like little bullets. That first night, I put them in as I finished my nightly reading in bed. I settled in for the night and my husband came in. I could barely hear anything. He sounded like the adults in a Peanuts cartoon.

I said (a few decibels too loud), "I can't hear you. I have these ear plugs in so I won't hear you snoring." He just kept talking, saying who knows what: "*Wah-wah-wah-wah-wahhhhh.*"

In the middle of the night, I got up to use the bathroom. When I came back to bed, my husband was snoring. Granted, I could barely hear it, but I could still hear it. Same rhythm. Same noises. The worst part of the ear plugs was that this was now *all* I could hear. There were no extraneous noises of the cat upstairs or the whistling noise the old refrigerator makes in the next room. That was all mercifully muffled out by the ear plugs, leaving only the muted *zzzzzz . . . puh!* of my sleeping husband.

As I lay there contemplating the pros and cons of hari-kari, wondering how fast I could buy a ritualistic sword on eBay, I must have fallen asleep anyway. Apparently muted snoring isn't as insomnia-producing as full-blown snoring.

My only concern now is whether or not these little green foamy things are reusable or not. The package label is unclear, but:

a) There are ten pairs in the package. Why would there be ten pairs if they were reusable? I'm trying not to think too hard about the alternative answers to this question. (*Oh, no she di'int.*)

b) I can't stop myself from wondering what kind of ear gunk gets on the little green foamy things—gunk I won't see because, well, they're foamy and they're . . . green.

I'm waiting for the day when this is the biggest problem in my day. Until then, it's back to my Internet research on the least painful forms of suicide. Just in case.   ♣

What Happened in Vegas

A Diary: Part Three

October 15, 2000

Night of the High Rollers, or Why I Won't Be Changing My Name to Bugsy Siegel Any Time Soon

Most of you have probably never been to Vegas (and certainly not to visit your parents), and therefore wouldn't realize that the "old" Las Vegas is really downtown Las Vegas, with Main Street as its, well, main street. The currently famous Vegas Strip is a several-mile long stretch of roadway called Las Vegas Boulevard. Up until last night we'd been concentrating most of our sightseeing to the Strip. Last night my folks took us all downtown to Fremont Street to see the shops and to view the Fremont Street Experience.

Fremont Street used to be a regular street popu-
lated with cars, but a few years ago they closed it off,
paved it over with new cement, set up outside kiosks,
and kept up the "traditional" casinos there (including
Vegas Vic and Sassy Sally, that neon cowboy guy and
gal seen in the movies). They also hoisted a huge canopy over the street—not a typical cloth canopy, but one
comprised of over two million light bulbs. These bulbs
are computer-programmed to change color and give
off different synchronized light shows (complete with
music) every hour.

It's one of the few situations where casinos volun-
tarily turn off the lights on their marquees, and that in
itself is saying something!

We got some splendid pictures last night, including
a doozy that I can't wait to post on my Web site. There
were three women walking around as living promo-
tions for some "girlie" show, dressing in neon-colored
skin-tight leather-like body suits, black bobbed-haircut
wigs, and *Matrix*-like sunglasses. I think they were each
about eight feet tall (their legs came up to my chin) and
wore size 2 bodysuits. (Then again, who would make
those bodysuits in size 18W anyway? That would have
to be against the law, wouldn't it?)

We bought a few souvenirs. (Doesn't everyone need
personalized Las Vegas condoms with a pair of dice on
the package? There are way too many jokes here about
taking chances and gambling, but I'm too genteel to
mention any of them. Except, I kind of just did.) My
folks took Gracie back to their place and left Wayne

and me to break the bank at a casino of our choosing. It was about nine-thirty P.M.

We had been mentally budgeting an "entertainment" amount of a certain dollar figure, assuming that we'd still be spending far less than most folks spend on vacations, and far less than even the price of going to the movies. The machines are fun, the "ping!" is pleasant, and frankly, the people-watching is better than anywhere in the world.

We ended up at a downtown casino called Fitzgerald's. There is a huge 3-D leprechaun on the side of the building, tipping his hat mechanically twenty-four hours a day and pointing toward a gaudily lit pot of gold at the end of the rainbow. It beckons you in. It entices you to get that pot of shiny gold.

However . . .

What they don't tell you is the obvious fact: The pot of gold is ON the building and not actually IN the slot machines.

Every casino has its own buffet, café, or restaurant—all designed with one goal in mind: to keep you from leaving. If you're hungry, they want you to eat there, at any loss to them financially, as long as you don't leave their doors to eat and probably never come back because you meandered into a different casino instead.

Fitzgerald's has an added distinction: It boasts its own McDonald's, complete with glitzy lights, of course. (Why there is an obviously Scottish restaurant like McDonald's in an Irish casino is beyond me.)

Wayne and I played nickel poker for a long time, sitting adjacent to the hourly *Tribute to Elvis* singer who'd serenade us all loudly with his renditions of "Love Me Tender," "Viva Las Vegas," and other things he assured us were Elvis songs. He looked the part. He sounded the part. But I could have done without the continuous gush of "This is only a tribute to 'The Kaannng' . . . No one can *really* imitate 'The Kaannng' . . . 'The Kaannng' is my idol and I don't pretend to be nearly as good as he was. . . ." And I think I also heard him mutter, "But do I have to wear the polyester jumpsuit with the fake love handles sewn in?"

More later in another section. . . . My dad is calling us to a dinner of grilled hot dogs and hamburgers. You can grill out all winter in Vegas.

Dad, thank you . . . *thankyouverymuch!*

Continued on page 91 . . .

Pennies in the Couch

Did you ever have one of those days where you spend inordinate amounts of time trying to save money? Clipping coupons, flipping through sale fly-ers, driving the extra ten miles to a better thrift store? Well, I seem to be having one of those *lifetimes*.

I freely admit that I brought this on myself. I'm a self-diagnosed underachieving genius. Actually, the genius part is self-diagnosed; the underachieving part is well-documented with empirical data. I came to grips with this tendency one day while I was still a single mom when I asked one of my sons to help me find some penny wrappers I'd stashed somewhere so we could wrap the stray pennies hidden around the house.

I tried to make the penny-hunt a game for my youngest daughter.

"Let's see who can find the most coins!" I said, thinking myself very clever until she scampered from her bedroom with her entire set of pogs, thinking they were coins.

My plan was to walk to the convenience store and annoy the clerk by paying for a jar of overpriced spaghetti sauce with rolls of pennies. I was at the mercy of the corner store that day because the car was in the shop with an expensive, debilitating illness—curable, but tragically, not until payday.

We didn't find enough change in the couch cushions—or the candy dish, or the junk drawer in the kitchen, or the pockets of my jeans, or the kids' jeans, or even in all the piggy banks in the house combined. And we never found the penny wrappers.

I thought, *How did I get into this predicament? I'm a bright girl—but here I am, typesetting business cards for a living and using paper napkins for the next thirty-six hours because we just ran out of toilet paper.*

In dire circumstances, I often want to leap immediately to the too-easy answer: "I must have done something wrong and God is punishing me." My mama taught me well, though, because when **other** folks are in dire circumstances, I never think ill of them. Instead, I weep with them, watch their faith grow and flourish under adversity, and admire them from afar. But when **I'm** the one in a bad way, I'm positive it's because I flubbed up big-time. This day was no exception.

As I ran down the steps, holding aloft the grimy quarter I'd found wedged in a corner of my room between the baseboard and the carpet, I wondered what my mother would say if she saw me like this. I had never wanted for anything as a child, and my parents were doing twice as well in their retirement as I was doing now in the prime of my scatter-brained life. Oh sure, I could blame my sorry financial state on the modest full-time job I was forced to hold after the unforeseen divorce, or on the distraction that comes with being back on the chopping block again and dating for the first time since the Reagan administration. There were plenty of places to shift the blame—and all my supportive friends would pat me on the back for my efforts as a single mom. I could easily dodge this shameful bullet.

Yet, as I searched the pantry for a stray can of decent vegetables I might have overlooked, and as I contemplated using the Hamburger Helper as a side dish without putting meat in it (which works, by the way), I decided to take the time to pray a little. God's always had interesting ways of getting my attention away from the mundane day-to-day stuff and back to Him where it belongs. He knows even better than I that self-inflicted poverty will get me every time. Prayer born of poverty refocuses one's perspective.

I stopped measuring the worth of my life by money that day. Good thing, too, since I didn't have any. I started measuring it by relationships—with God first, then with family, then with others. Was I communicating with God? Was I teaching my kids by word and example? Was I faithful in the little things? (Answer key available upon request.) There was plenty lacking in my life that needed even more attention than the pantry or the car or learning to decipher a bus schedule again.

I said grace that evening at a dinner of cheap chicken salad sandwiches, Zesty Italian Three-Cheese Hamburger Helper minus the hamburger, and half a bag of miraculously un-freezer-burned frozen corn heated and slathered with cheap margarine and salt. The kids were happy—these were some of their favorites, and to them this was better than the fancier roast beef and vegetable dinner I would rather have served them.

Seeing the simple smiles on their unknowing faces, it was easy to be thankful for God's many blessings— again.   ❖

Say Ahhh!

I obsessively checked my e-mail for the umpteenth time. Keeping in contact with friends and family across the globe was a cinch with e-mail. I had become the E-Mail Queen. Nothing could distract me now.

My toddler came to my desk and began to play doctor with me using her play-doctor kit. She tested me for all sorts of disorders, the names of which I didn't recognize as they tumbled out of her preschool mouth. She grabbed a fat pink thermometer and poked around inside my ear as I typed. When she hit a sensitive spot, I jerked my head away from her and asked, "Addie, what are you doing?"

She blinked at me, looked into my ear, shook her head, and said, "Mommy, I'm going to have to take your brain out now."

I balked, then chuckled and went back to my online mission field. She climbed onto the footrest of my chair and took my face in her hands.

It might have become a poignant mother-daughter moment, if only she hadn't whipped my head to one side and stared into my eardrum again, hoping to find something—*anything!*

She planted herself between me and my keyboard. I heard "You've got mail!" wafting from the computer speakers, but was powerless. I sighed, trying to ignore the urgent sounds of the computer.

I spoke to her as she continued her poking and peering. "You have to take my brain out? Why?"

She rolled her big blue toddler eyes at me. "Because you're done with it."

Was it that obvious?   ♣

I'm Hoping You'll See Less of Me

Diet Diary: I'm down eight pounds so far, having gone up two pounds over the holiday season for reasons I can only blame on everyone around me:

• The neighbor brought over homemade cookies.

• My mother gave me a non-refundable gift certificate to a Chinese buffet.

• There was a one-pound chocolate bar in my stocking. At least I *think* it was my stocking.

• That eggnog poured itself down my throat when I wasn't looking.

And the list of credible excuses goes on.

I will allow myself one real excuse: It is impossible for the woman of the house to go on a diet unless she takes everyone else down with her. And I doubt anyone in my house is willing to take a bullet (or a celery stalk) for me. This time I'm on my own . . . but I still have to cook for everyone else. And, in my case, "everyone else" includes one teenager on a sugar-free diet, another teenager on a sugar-free *low-carb* diet, yet another who comes into the house just long enough to drink a gallon of milk in one gulp, and a man who eats anything I put in front of him as long as he doesn't have to cook it or clean up after it . . . or even put his own one lousy plate in the dishwasher after he's done inhaling the food like a shop-vac. But I digress.

This is a huge dilemma, the kind of dilemma someone like me—with no will power of my own and no inclination to borrow someone else's—cannot bear for very long without dire consequences. Consequences like eating a Quarter Pounder and washing it down with a Starbucks Frappuccino, followed by a pack of Ho-Ho's.

Some days I fight the urge to yell, "That's it! You're all on your own!" and enact that declaration as house law for the next year and a half. But what kind of eating lessons would I be teaching myself if I could lose weight only when I have to cook for no one but myself? Easy enough when you're *single*, but tack on a handful of teenagers with metabolisms running at twice the speed of light and a husband who never met a Hot Pocket he didn't like, and you have a diet disaster in the making.

Part of one diet group I recently signed up for involved a periodic two-day "cleansing" that severely limited my caloric intake and flushed my system by forcing me to drink their pre-made fruity-juicy stuff and eating some veggies and lean protein. At the time, this seemed like a good idea for jumpstarting a diet that had plateaued. And, aside from the pulse-pounding headaches and mind-blackening nausea I developed midway through Day One, it worked. Oh sure, I could have done without the flop-sweats and the LSD-like hallucinations, but you can't have everything. In fact, on this diet, you can't have *anything*.

Plus, I have a feeling that any day now they're going to modify that two-day cleansing plan into something like this: "Drink 45 glasses of water today and breathe only our bottled, purified air, available for $49.95. Breathing regular air may result in bloating, weight gain, indigestion, insomnia, and copious amounts of hair loss—but not necessarily from your head."

Be afraid. Be very afraid.

And pass the Twinkies.   ❖

Household Chores

(a poem written in childhood)

I helped my mother in the house,
It gave me such delight!
Until I found out soon enough
I could do nothing right.

We first cleaned up the living room
And watched the vacuum clog
Because I turned it up on "high"
And then sucked up the dog.

Next we cleaned the bathroom up,
And, boy, I surely blushed
'Cause Mother's arm was still inside
When I the toilet flushed.

Next we ironed the wrinkled clothes,
Which started out just grand,
Until I set the iron down
And burned my mother's hand.

I never do those household chores,
Not since that day back then.
Mom said she'd do those things to *me*
If I ever "helped" again!

What Happened in Vegas

A Diary: Part Four, Elvis Edition

October 17, 2000

Today is a great day if you find yourself bored at five-thirty P.M. Eastern time, have Internet access, and want something unique to do online.

Come to the wedding chapel's Web site and click on the LIVE webcast! There you'll see Wayne and me renewing our wedding vows with Elvis!

What better way to wind down a whirlwind and wonderful vacation than to experience something Vegas is known for? (No, not the buffets—we've been hitting those all week!)

It is T-minus two hours till the limousine arrives to take us to the Elvis wedding chapel, and Wayne still doesn't have a clue what's about to happen. (That's probably just as well. If he did, he'd have taken a cab to Arizona by now.)

LATER:

And look, I'm posting a picture of us in our nuptial re-wedded bliss . . . .

Continued on page 105 . . .

Is Nyquil a Legal Drug?

I had been sick with The World's Worst Head Cold® (which was so bad I trademarked it) for over two weeks, which truly changed my outlook from *I Love Life* cheeriness to *Let Me Please Just Die Overnight, Okay? Anything But This Incessant Coughing and Wheezing*. Really, quite a change in personality for me, often talkative to a fault. In fact, when my throat hurt its worst, I sat next to Wayne, who was asking me something innocuous (as is his habit).

I squeaked out quietly, "Throat . . . hurts . . . too . . . much. . . . I . . . can't . . . talk." In his usual droll fashion, he continued to stare at the TV, now playing another old episode of *Alias Smith and Jones*, and said simply, "Finally."

A few days later, just as I was getting better, he

started sneaking the thermometer out of the medicine cabinet and getting up in the middle of the night to hit the Chloraseptic bottle. He obviously had a problem and needed an intervention. Unlike regular people, Wayne unscrews the spritzy top of the spray bottle and just chugs the stuff like a shot of cheap bourbon, gargling it loudly right outside our bedroom door—awakening even the mice in the basement—and then swallows it. The sound is more effective than the trays of mousey poison we put down near the fridge. (The trays have this blue crunchy stuff in them and look like little pet food dishes—almost cruel, really, except when you consider the alternative of mice crunching on the Cap'n Crunch in our pantry.)

Where was I? Head colds. Wayne was now fighting off the cold I probably gave him. Probably? Considering I was sleeping in his recliner and preparing his dinner and doing his laundry for the two weeks I was sick, yeah, I'd say he got it from me. Anyway, he must know what a turn-on the mixed aroma of Nyquil and hand sanitizer is because he started dousing himself in both things like they were cheap cologne on a gigolo. I swear he uses the pump-bottle of hand sanitizer like body wash in the shower. Reminds me fondly of when we were first dating and he'd wedge a quart-sized pump-bottle of the stuff between the bucket seats of his car and use it before kissing me at the drive-in—back when we were middle-aged and foolish!

Maybe I should let him suffer with that cold. He's earned it.   ♣

Water, Water Everywhere

By the time I was 38, I had still lived a relatively sheltered life. I'd never gone streaking, never given blood (on purpose), and never slept in a waterbed. Then I married a man who owns a king-sized waterbed — and since then it's been sink or swim.

Getting *into* the bed is easy. Let's just say "stop, drop and roll" works for more than just fire safety. But climbing *out* is a different matter. No amount of unladylike gymnastics or contortions can get me out of that bed gracefully. And the padded side rails aren't good for anything except moral support. Or a rather unseemly dismount. Mary Lou Retton, I'm not.

My husband's quite used to sailing the seven seas at bedtime and doesn't need to take Dramamine before docking himself at night. Plus, he's fourteen inches taller than I am and—unlike me—doesn't need a pool ladder and a life guard to get in and out of the bed. Meanwhile, on my side of the bed, falling asleep with loud sloshing noises in my ears does nothing for my bladder. So I wake up in the middle of the night and sway back and forth, trying to hoist myself over the side and onto the floor. The mattress, which is filled with more water than the Hoover Dam sees in a year, lurches to and fro and wakes him up.

"Do you need a little *push* or something?" he mumbles from the inlet on his side of the bed.

"No."

"Life preserver?"

"No. Now go back to sleep."

"Wet suit? Rubber ducky? A copy of *Moby Dick*?"

I ignore him and create a small tsunami trying to get out of the bed.

"What are you *doing* over there?" he mumbles.

"The breast stroke."

"Need any help?"

"Very funny. No!"

I don't know whether to kiss him or drown him.

"How can you get comfortable in this contraption every night?" I ask.

"Easy," he says. "You're good ballast."

Drown him. Definitely drown him.   ❖

The Bus Stops Here

I'm sitting on a bench at the busway, minding my own business, trying to act like I instinctively know the bus schedule by heart and do this all the time. But, I know better. I know my Honda is in the shop and this is the first time I've taken the bus in decades. And now I need to maneuver my way via bus schedule and self-induced panic across town to the shop to pick up the car.

While others around me are nonchalantly chatting or doing other things, I'm worried I'll get on the wrong bus, or get on the right bus but get off at the wrong stop. I secretly remind myself to buy a better car, as soon as I find several thousand dollars in loose change in the couch cushions.

In the distance, still blocks away, a bus that will probably stop here rounds the corner and pops into view. For the umpteenth time, my hand dives into my purse and finds the zippered inside pocket where I keep quarters and dimes. Going in this direction, out of town, I pay the fare when I get *off* the bus—I think. I check again to see if I have enough change, worried that I have inexplicably forgotten how to count money and will get on the bus without enough money to pay for the trip. I have no clue what they do to people who get on the bus without the proper fare. Does the driver make an added stop at the next police station so the cops can cuff them when they make a break for it? Could a person end up with a police record for this? I shake myself awake and pay more attention.

As I ponder these deep truths, the bus gets within a block of where I'm standing. I look up just in time to see it stop right in front of me. What if I'm wrong and they now collect fares upon entering the bus? The pressure is too great. I'm not ready.

I step aside to let others get on the bus ahead of me so I can watch what they do. I've become a mindless bus sheep. An older lady—clearly a senior citizen who rides free anyway—gets on first, which doesn't help me determine at what point fares are paid. The second person in line is the middle-aged man I saw spitting on the ground when I first got to the bus stop. He walks right past the bus driver and the fare box without dropping in any money or showing any sort of bus pass, so I figure we're paying upon exit, as I suspected. My heartbeat slows to a rate that might not need a pacemaker after all.

My hand slowly slides back out of my purse as I take my turn and step onto the bus, where my next worry assaults me: Is there an appropriate seat left for me? I've been so busy worrying about the method and timing of bus fare payment that I neglected to allow enough angst-time to deal with the implications of having nowhere to sit, or having to sit with people who make me nervous or scared or who just creep me out. I'm suddenly aware of all the issues I still have. I realize I am a pathetic blob of fear and self-loathing.

I look around me as I settle into an empty seat on the aisle halfway to the back. Before I have time to chastise myself for being such a panic-stricken idiot about something so simple, the bus turns left at the next intersection and heads south.

But the mechanic's shop is north.   ♣

I'm Your Biggest Fan

My beloved husband has to tinker with every electrical object within a fifty-mile radius of his toolbox. It's his nature. But for some reason this doesn't include our four ceiling fans. He avoids them like the plague. And I'm pretty sure he routinely avoids the plague.

At some point during the Mezzazoic Era the chain on the living room fan broke and now we can't turn it off. In the summer Wayne says, "It provides good circulation." In the winter he says, "It brings warm air off the ceiling." (And whooshes it out the front door at breakneck speed, I might add.)

The whole contraption wiggles around in an electronic belly-dance. Wayne says, "I should balance that thing," and spends half a weekend at Walmart buying a balancing kit, which he puts on the coffee table and promptly forgets.

One time he shut off the electric to fix something — and the fan finally stopped. The dust gunk on the paddles was a foot thick. I thought I might be able to use it to stuff pillows for the couch but hosed it off with a power washer instead.

The ceiling fan in our home office tries to shear off the top of my head whenever I get too close. It's a good thing I'm only five-foot-two, or by now I'd be, well, probably five-foot-one. When this fan goes into its own little belly-dance, Wayne says, "I gotta balance that thing," and disappears on a field trip to Home Depot to buy another balancing kit, which he puts on the coffee table alongside the first one. I make a mental note to get a bigger coffee table.

The ceiling fan for the kitchen has been in the box since 1997. When the coffee table fills up with gadgets, faucet parts and balancing kits, we start using the kitchen fan box as an auxiliary coffee table.

Finally Wayne finds time to install that fan. (He has no excuses this time. It came with its own balancing kit.) This one does only a *tiny* belly-dance. I feel strangely blessed.

The bedroom ceiling fan — which hangs directly over our waterbed — is a mystery to me. One of the paddles is inexplicably bent and hangs at an awkward angle. In hushed tones, Wayne cautions me *never* to turn it on. *Never.* Whenever I enter the room, my fingers are drawn to the switch out of morbid curiosity.

But I resist the urge, because ever since he said that I've had nightmares of burning helicopters spinning out of control and crashing into Lake Erie.   ♣

What Happened in Vegas

A Diary: Part Five

October 18, 2000

We're hours away from leaving for the airport to come home. We'll probably be on Pacific Time till at least February. Beyond that, we'll have no excuse for our behavior, I guess.

A white stretch limousine arrived at the house yesterday at two P.M. to take us the short distance to the wedding chapel to renew our vows. Wayne was napping (okay, *snoring*) till the limo arrived, so he spent most of the ceremony in a confused daze—just like our original wedding. (Today he hopes it was just a dream. I may let him continue to think that. It's less embarrassing for him.)

I'd never been in a stretch limo before. Inside were a TV, VCR, champagne glasses and decanters (empty, though, in our case, because I was too cheap to pay the extra fee), and plush leather seats. We were met inside the door of the chapel by Elvis himself. He was handsomely decked out in a fire-engine red, sequined, bell-bottomed jumpsuit, and had jet-black sideburns and swept-back hair. The phone rang, and the receptionist was busy with our paperwork, so he nonchalantly answered the phone. Who knew Elvis was so down-to-earth? So accessible to the common man. So . . . secretarial.

We had to sign release forms for the live webcast. Wayne balked a bit, asked how much he'd get paid for his performance, but then finally signed. (I left him no choice.) I heard him mumble something about a trip to Reno later, but dismissed it as sleepiness.

We were then shown into the chapel and Elvis showed us how to go through the motions smoothly. He pointed out the video camera (for our personal videotape), and the Web camera. (We waved a few times for anyone who was watching. People do log on there randomly and watch, so we don't know who saw it.) Sadly, we began the ceremony about ten minutes before our prearranged time, so I have no idea if people missed it because of that. Plus, there was the whole RealPlayer fiasco. Don't get me started.

THE HOSS CHALLENGE:

Today we got a request from Wayne. He decided that he wanted to go back to Timber's and try their Hoss Burger Challenge. If you remember, that's the

2½–3-pound burger as big as a dinner plate, complete with tons of tomatoes, lettuce, cheese, sauce, etc. The challenge was to eat two (yes, two) of these monsters in half an hour (yes, half). He had to eat every bit, including the condiments and bun. He had to sit at a separate table from anyone else and be timed by the staff (synchronized down to the second). The prize for this is $100, both burgers free, and your photo on their Hall of Fame board.

He was allowed to do any cutting or arranging beforehand, but couldn't take any bites till he was told to. He cut the burgers into quarters and got everything arranged.

GO!

He was right on schedule for the first half of the first burger, which had to take no more than 7½ minutes. But, he was at the 16-minute mark at the end of Burger 1, so we feared the worst.

We didn't know what to do. Should we cheer him on, ignore him and talk in hushed tones behind his back, or go sit in the car and pray that he not explode? We opted for sitting there normally, but trying vainly to ignore him. He didn't say much of anything, didn't even look at us till he hit the end of Burger 1 at 16 minutes. *Uh-oh.*

Things kinda went downhill from there. Chaos ensued, and all hell broke loose. My memory might be a bit off, but I vaguely remember someone losing consciousness, a small tow-truck, paramedics, the fire department, a crane, several two-ton girders, and

someone saying, "Don't go toward the light, Wayne
. . . don't go toward the light!"

Well, okay, maybe I'm exaggerating. But he did realize that it wasn't gonna happen, and he (thankfully)
slowed the pace and tried instead to save face and not
get too sick for the car ride back home. It probably didn't
help when we stopped at a store in the 85-degree desert
sun, and everyone but him ran in "just for a minute" to
pick up some trashy novels and word puzzle books for
the flight back. We came back out to the car and found
Wayne with the seatback reclined fully, cooking there
sunny-side up, looking a little green around the gills.

To add insult to injury, the construction workers
here in the neighborhood laid new curb all around my
parents' block today, and we had to "walk the plank"
across a small board to get from the wide wet cement
into the driveway. Wayne (and the 1½ burgers he was
carrying around with him) somehow made it across
the board safely.

Later that evening, Wayne and I braved sitting at a
blackjack table with a real Las Vegas dealer. We sat at
the "cheapskate" $5 bet tables with the other embar-
rassingly-low bettors, and decided to take it all in as
a once-in-a-lifetime experience. I'm a people-watcher,
and this is a unique city in which to watch people from
all over the world in various weird places and situations.

Blackjack is an easier game to play because it doesn't
force you to bet against other people, and there aren't
nearly as many subtle nuances and body language as in

a game like poker. We sat at the same table and made a few minimum bets and played well. We watched other people come and go from our table. The people who sat down were as varied as I've ever seen. Most were very friendly, and I found that the tables are often a place to socialize with people while you're playing (or watching other people play).

I came away from this experience with an odd fascination about how the tables work: the lengthy list of rules, the plethora of "eye in the sky" cameras that watch everyone's moves all the time, and how very different each casino is in atmosphere and type of person frequenting it.

The tables change dealers every hour or so, and every time a dealer leaves your table or arrives, he/she has to show both hands, palms up and then down, to the camera. I thought this was just a neat little gesture of hello or goodbye until Wayne explained that it was to show that the dealer wasn't filching a chip or two out of the tray. Dishonest people in Las Vegas? Who knew? Once you place your bet, you're not allowed to touch your chips. At most casinos, you never touch the cards. You can tip a dealer outright if you wish, or you can "ride" a tip with your bet and the dealer can then end up doubling the tip (or the house gets it if your hand loses).

It seems to be a nice gesture to tip a dealer if you are dealt a blackjack or two, and tips are usually a $1 coin/ token. I don't understand this gesture, since the casino insists that the dealer isn't cheating and isn't handing you that blackjack on purpose, and yet most people tip dealers for those blackjacks after the fact. Superstition runs rampant in this town, even among civilized, intelligent people. Sitting in an oddly lit casino, with no windows and no clocks, for hours on end must change a person. You do silly things like tip supposedly impartial dealers for giving you cards they have no control over.

There were enough things to notice in these places to keep me fascinated for ages. We met people from all over the country, and the dealers are from all over the world. We saw nametags such as:

"Hi, I'm Anna, from Russia."

"Hi, I'm Joe, from Chicago."

"Hi, I'm Wei, from China."

"Hi, I'm Feng, from Taiwan."

"Hi, I'm Amy, from Las Vegas."

Hi, we're Wayne and Linda, from Pittsburgh. Didn't have quite the same ring to it.

I have a strange feeling there are a few short stories buried in this week's experiences. It's another world in there, and seeing the Strip at night is something one never forgets. (Fifteen thousand miles of neon tubing isn't easily missed.)

Well, Gracie just came in from using her grandpa's push broom to sweep the eternal desert dust off the driveway. Apparently this type of ritualistic sweeping is done throughout the house all the time. The kitchen can get swept up to three times a day on breezier days, even with a good screen door.

We're going to visit with my folks now. We'll be leaving for McCarran Airport in a little while. Did you know that a jet dumps more suckers . . . I mean, *people* . . . into this town every two-and-a-half minutes? The thought of all those unsuspecting people descending on the Strip day and night, 24/7, is sobering. We certainly don't have people rushing into Pittsburgh like that. (Hey, once we have two new stadiums, though, who knows?)

We leave the west (and the nice weather and majestic mountains) behind, and return to the end of autumn's colors and roads that actually curve and go uphill and down once in a while. We will be happy to be home, but a little sad that the week has gone by so quickly. As the wind whips through our tousled hair . . .

Oh, wait—that's from the trashy novel I bought to read on the plane. Never mind.   ❖

Close Encounters with Mark Spitz

It happens to every girl at some point—some are younger, some older, but all of us succumb to it eventually. Yes, of course, I'm talking about puberty. That once-in-a-lifetime event that is exciting and glorious for about six or seven minutes and then becomes a colossal hassle for the next forty years.

In my particular case, I was thirteen when I entered the wonderful world of womanhood (not to be confused with the Wonderful World of Disney, which I also entered when I was thirteen, but that was a family vacation to Florida and not related to this in the slightest). After all the hubbub created by my nursing-school-trained mother when I was ten (complete with medical textbooks and graphs and charts and the ensuing panic at the obvious grotesque *lies* she was telling me about where babies come from), the actual event that summer day was anticlimactic. Some pad company had recently come out with the newfangled "mini-pad" (which my mother deemed "cute!" when she first saw them), and we were already stocked up and prepared. And, once I got her to stop brooding and clucking over me like a mother hen, everything was fine—and even boring compared to the earlier hype.

It was, though, summertime, and at our house that meant daily treks to the local community swimming pool from about noon till four P.M. Despite the recent developments, I tagged along that day, not wanting to miss the socializing, even if I would have to miss the swimming. I hadn't realized just how much of a typical pool day was taken up by actual swimming, though, until we got there and within fifteen minutes I was bored of hanging out near our towels on our spot on the grass.

A little while later, I offered to trek up the hill to the snack bar, and, laden with coinage, I broke out of my towel-sitting boredom and made the voyage, expecting to return laden with gifts of fried food and cold soda. The lines at the snack bar were always long, so I figured this would kill a fair amount of time. And boy, was I right.

As I inched up the line slowly, the July heat began to beat down on me, even under the canopy roof over the snack bar area. To this day, I don't know if it was the heat, the humidity, or the bodily events to which I was not yet accustomed, but when I was finally going to be the next customer waited upon, everything in my field of vision began to look strangely like a photo negative. Colors were turned inside out, and if I hadn't known myself to be a naive, thirteen-year-old total goody-two-shoes from suburbia, I'd have thought I was high on something psychedelic.

Sadly, I would have been mistaken about that, but it might have had a less embarrassing ending. Instead, the person working the counter asked me what I wanted, and I do not remember answering. I remember someone else asking me if I was all right, while everyone swam in a sea of inverted color and sound became muffled as if underwater. I vaguely remember falling backwards and thinking about the concrete floor on which I was standing at the time. You see, I had this way of ending up in the hospital every single summer with stitches in my head. Would this be the day for the summer of 1974?

Apparently not, as I next found myself calmly and safely staring up at the canopy roof, lying flat on the hard concrete, with no pain and with colors where they should be. Someone behind me in the long line must have caught me as I fell backwards. Someone else was telling everyone that I was coming around, and I managed to sit up on my own. Kind of.

The next thing I remember was lying flat on my back again, this time in a smaller, cooler room, on a small cot. My mother was next to me—I could hear her voice. When I opened my eyes fully and focused them, I gazed upon the gorgeous face of what had to be Mark Spitz. He was tan, with sleek black hair, wearing only a small bathing suit, and had a whistle around his neck, and he was hovering just a few inches from my face, peering into my eyes with curiosity and concern.

"Are you all right?" he breathed, taking my hand in his and expressing genuine care even through his perfect eyebrows and thick black mustache. "I'm the pool manager. You fainted."

I sighed. Of course I fainted. And I felt as if I might faint again! If this was what womanhood was like, no wonder they kept giving us pamphlets about it in school to prepare us. No one could have prepared me for this, not even my mother and her medical charts. Especially not the medical charts.

I batted my eyelashes a few times and let "Mark" help me sit up on the cot, my mother still hovering nearby like a traffic helicopter at rush hour. *Mother, don't you have a fifteen-minute-adult-swim to get to?*

And, just as I was about to breathe my heartfelt thanks to Mark and bat my eyelashes some more, my mother—helpful to a fault—blurted out behind him: "She'll be fine. She just got her first period today, and she must have felt a little lightheaded."

And with those simple words, my foray into womanhood ended and I was pushed back into childhood for a little while longer. Mark Spitz was going to have to wait.   ♣

O Sing of Spring!

(a poem written in adulthood)

The song is sung
That Spring has sprung . . .
And yet I have my doubt.

I'll hold my tongue
While Spring is young
While others sing and shout.

As bells are rung
And streamers hung
I sit alone and pout.

And I, high-strung,
My arms outflung,
Would rather not sit out.

Why fill a lung
With air that's wrung
With pollen that'll sprout?

The vines that clung
Their arms among
The sidewalk's stony grout

Have long since brung
Their curls hamstrung
While reaching up and out.

And farmer's dung
On pitchfork swung
Leaves odors all about.

And bees that stung!
And cows' bluetongue!
Well . . . I'm just not that devout.

And so I'll spout
That Spring's a lout
And leave your Spring unsung.

Dead Ringer

I was minding my own business, spending a glorious weekend with girlfriends from high school at a lovely cottage in Maryland, when an ominous thing happened. I felt a pinch at the base of one of the fingers of my left hand—a sharp little pain any time I bent a finger. One glance at my hand, one twist of my wedding ring revealed a split in the gold—all the way through the ring—and the angled edge of the metal caused by the rift was now pinching my finger. The thing looked like someone had snipped it with a pair of scissors.

My wedding ring was broken.

I was dumbfounded that the gold could just, well, break. Especially without my catching it on anything or hooking it on a knob or a handle or something. Did I just not know my own strength?

Despite the fact that my husband and I had brought six children from our previous marriages into our own marriage ten years earlier, and had therefore been ridiculously frugal about the money we spent getting married, it was time to start regretting the pennypinching decision to purchase our matching simple wedding bands at Walmart. Either that or God was punishing me for that getaway weekend with three women I'd gone through puberty with thirty-five years earlier. Nah, that couldn't be it.

Upon returning home, I took the ring to a jeweler, who soldered it for fifteen bucks—a figure I balked at only because it was fifty percent of the original cost of the ring. But, once I got the ring back, a week after our tenth anniversary, I was happy to be able to wear it and bend my fingers without puncture wounds or severe chafing and weeping and gnashing of teeth . . .

. . . until it happened again a month later. Either the jeweler used substandard solder (honestly, though, how substandard would it have to be to be worse than the Walmart ring itself?), or I had some pretty strong joints on my left hand. Or, God really was punishing me for something. I tried not to think about that pack of Twinkies I'd had last night . . . or the forty-two pairs of shoes in my closet. After all, what good would finger-pointing do now?

I had a decision to make: One option was to take the ring to a different jeweler to have it soldered again without having to explain why I was back. But if this kept happening, I'd quickly run out of jewelers. Plus, who knew if these people talked amongst themselves about their customers—at some sort of solderers convention or something? I couldn't take the chance.

The only other option was to buy myself another ring—one I could use as an "everyday" ring, saving the original for special occasions—but none of the Walmarts in the area had that ring in my size anymore. And besides, I had visions of this happening to a new ring all over again in a few years. No, Walmart was out, and so were K-Mart and Aldi's and Dollar General. I was going to have to spend some serious cash this time. My thirty-year class reunion was coming up in a week, so for that one night I purchased a cheapie metal-looking ring set (which came with a gargantuan "engagement ring") for nine bucks. Coupled with the fake plastic wedding band, I wore my real diamond (which was more sturdily built and was *not* purchased at a Walmart or a thrift store or through the Pennysaver), and no one at the reunion was the wiser.

After the reunion, I purchased a sturdy wedding band—one that will stand the test of time, which is far more lovely a symbol for our love and marriage than the idea of a ring that splits up every time you get too close.

This new ring cost me twice what the original ring cost, and I admit I got it on Amazon.com—but it's doing the job nicely so far. Not a nick or scratch on it, and certainly no gaping holes. There's a good reason for this durability, though: The thing weighs a ton and is made of tungsten carbide, which, according to the Amazon seller, is four times stronger than titanium.

I've learned some valuable lessons in this situation:

• The ring's heavy, sturdy weight on my finger means I'll never forget it's there and accidentally catch it on whatever broke the first one (like, a stiff wind or something). However, my ring finger now has six-pack abs from the added weight it's carrying around.

• If Wayne and I have a serious, horrible, nasty, vindictive fight, and I'm losing, I can threaten to bonk him on the head with the ring. That'll get his attention.

• New Valentine's Day slogan: "Nothing says love like tungsten carbide!"

• And last, what God—and the local jeweler—have joined together, let no man put asunder . . .   ♣

Random Things I Notice

Part of my job as a writer is to notice stuff. Stuff you just don't have the time or inclination to notice yourself. I care about you so much, dear reader, that I carry around a little black notebook so I can jot things down as I see them — so I won't forget them later. (And, at my age, forgetting them later means in about five minutes, when I get distracted by something major like the phone ringing or a piece of lint in my pants pocket.)

I dug out the little black notebook today and now realize that the list of random crap has gotten a little unwieldy. That can only mean that it's time to offload it from the notebook into the real book. (For those of you in public school, that means this book.) For your reading pleasure, of course. It's an important service I provide, and I'm only too happy to help you out as you struggle to remember this stuff buried in your busy days.

List #1: General Do's and Don'ts (Mostly Don'ts):

• **Don't** say "I'll have what she's having" unless you are absolutely sure you know what she's having.

• **Don't** fall in love with an ax murderer. And, as a helpful hint here: This starts by ignoring any communications containing the words "prison" and "penpal." This is a good place to start. After that, you're on your own.

• **Don't** let a husband with no sense of time start a major remodeling project. You know, one that involves items such as drywall or insulation. Or even a hammer. And this "don't" includes, in no uncertain terms, a husband with no sense of humor. Or one with no sense of danger. Or aesthetics. Or even one whose personal motto is, "It was on clearance." Trust me. I know what I'm talking about.

• **Don't** keep using the hot sauce if your ears start sweating.

• **Don't** irk a friend when she's majorly pregnant. She's busy growing a whole 'nother human being, and it apparently takes up a lot of brain space. She'll get that brain space back in a few decades, so be patient. ♣

Like Sands Through the Hourglass . . .

When I think back now on my mom watching *Days of Our Lives* when I was a child, I wonder why she ever had the show on. It's not her style to be that frivolous with her viewing time (although now she watches *Diners, Drive-Ins and Dives* and *Meerkat Manor* and some show where dog catchers break into people's houses with big sticks and find cockroaches everywhere *every single time*—you know, shows for the high-IQed among us). And she's never been one for drama in real life, let alone in her TV-viewing life. So, what was the appeal for a reasonably sane woman such as my mother?

When I was in college, I noticed that everyone watched soap operas—you know, when they should have been in class or studying or both. (This is the most likely explanation for my sudden dip from A's in high school to C's in my freshman year at Carnegie-Mellon. Well, this, and the fact that I scheduled early morning lectures on the significance of ancient history on modern teenagers—lectures where attendance was never taken. Lesson learned.)

Again, what was the appeal? There aren't many of these dinosaur series left (*Days of Our Lives* remains one of the stalwart holdouts, with the occasional visit by matriarch Alice Horton on the Christmas shows every year), and yet the popularity of these shows was enormous at the time. And *Days of Our Lives* has been around since 1965—a whopping forty-five years as of this writing.

But again, why so long? Why the popularity? I put forth the premise that the popularity of these outrageous shows (and their present-day counterparts) is because they are precisely *so* far removed from the reality of our everyday lives. Let's face it: When a character on one of these shows is facing a brain-lung-heart transplant and has double-amnesia and a husband who's sleeping with her evil twin, it's bound to make your own life look a little better by comparison. That flat tire on the freeway just doesn't hold the same kind of drama (unless you're on Facebook Mobile).

Let's take a small peek into the days of their lives, through the medium of ridiculously rhetorical questions. Remember, there are no right or wrong answers. (That's why they're rhetorical.)

• Can anyone say or do anything incriminating on these shows without the wrong person conveniently standing in an adjacent doorway listening? And misunderstanding?

• Why does everyone hang out at the local hospital as if it were a Starbucks? Isn't that just a little creepy?

• Who would keep living in a town where there are routine kidnappings and murders by long-lost siblings or people with multiple personalities and/or adult-onset amnesia?

• Why do the middle-aged people never age, but infants can go from diapers in one episode to college in another episode a month later?

• Why is a character being pregnant a huge deal—fraught with DNA and paternity tests and all manner of prenatal complications, getting major attention every second of that character's existence—but as soon as the baby is born, the mother is never seen taking care of it or changing a diaper or being stuck at home with a colicky baby, unable to get enough sleep or to even shower regularly or eat hot food again? You know, like the rest of us. . . .

• And why does that same baby conveniently disappear from view but yet it shows up again two years later as a pregnant teen in search of her own real father? *Who does the math on these shows?*

• Why does nobody work at a McDonald's? Or eat at one? Everyone eats at the one restaurant in town, which is owned by one of the characters, who never has to actually work there.

• Why do these people have way too much time to sit in cafés (and hospitals) talking about other people's problems? And why do their schedules conveniently dovetail with one another just in time to sit around discussing these problems at the right moments? Doesn't anybody have a job with regular hours—except for doctors, who apparently live at the hospital? Seriously, though, can you blame them? That's where the whole town is most of the time anyway.

• Why do we never see anyone cleaning the toilet or throwing out moldy food from the fridge? Or taking out the trash? Or doing the laundry—unless it's a suspicious woman who conveniently finds something incriminating in her husband's pants pockets while checking them before doing the laundry?

• Why does everyone in town go to the same church, which is incredibly nondenominational to the point of absurdity and has about three pews? Why is it no bigger than the hospital chapel, where a character can go to pray and change the plot so that whatever he or she prays for actually happens—usually within minutes of praying for it? Does anyone in real life actually know where their hospital chapel is?

• Why do none of the other characters notice when a character leaves the show and comes back later played by a different actor? Don't any of them have the urge to yell, "Good grief, Daphne, what happened to your face? And, didn't you used to be a redhead? And a man?"

As I mull over these gross writing *faux pas*—with an odd mixture of revulsion and envy—I'm led to believe that my own novels don't stand a snowball's chance in hell of publication. And, my daydreams of one day being a successful television script writer are forever dashed, because there's no way I could come up with plot garbage that's simultaneously that ridiculous and sublime. I'd have to drink myself into a stupor or eat a few dozen Krispy Kremes and send myself into a diabetic coma in order to maintain the heightened sense of awareness necessary to write episodes to rival what I've seen on these shows over the years.

But, at least I've got something to shoot for as a writer. It's good to have goals.   ❖

Hell on Wheels

It's a story I've told my kids a hundred times. "Tell us about the skating rink when you were a kid, Mom!" They're all grown now, but they still love hearing about that skating rink. What makes the story so much fun is that you just can't make up stuff like this. I swear it's all true, but I'm not sure the kids believe me in their politically correct, lawsuit-happy world.

In the 1970s, everyone in my elementary school had a skating party at the local skating rink—often around our tenth birthdays, which is when I had mine. We all took the rink's many quirks in stride, not knowing any better and not having the perspective of age or wisdom. Especially wisdom. So, none of us thought anything of asking the front desk clerk and owner, ancient and tiny Ma Long, for our size skates for each two-hour party rental, only to be handed a pair of skates that looked like something Cro-Magnon Man would have used had he invented the wheel a little sooner. The leather was always worn, the wheels were misshapen and some funky, faded color we couldn't identify, and the laces were frayed and missing the aglets necessary to lace them up properly. I spent hours at birthday parties sitting in the anteroom of the skating rink, with skates already on my feet, trying to get those frayed laces through those dozens and dozens of holes in the leather. I can see us all now, lined up on the benches, licking our fingers and trying to use the spit to twist and twirl the lace ends to get them through those stubborn holes. Thinking about the germs we must have ingested doing this makes me ill now, in a retroactive sort of way.

Once our skates were on, we'd get up and sway and wobble our way to the railing, watching the other kids already skating around the wooden floor of the oblong rink. Getting into the flow of traffic was like merging onto the turnpike at rush hour in a Chevette with a burned-out clutch, but somehow we all managed to get onto the rink in one piece. I usually ended up doing a butt-kiss with the floor within the first trip around the rink, but at least I always had company. If I was lucky, I'd start a chain-reaction and ten of us would end up sprawled on the floor together, with everyone forgetting just who started it. It soon became clear that the inexperienced skaters had to find a way to cut across traffic and head into the empty center of the rink. But cutting across traffic was taking your life into your hands.

Two features of this particular rink stand out in my mind: the music and the bathrooms. The music playing over the antique speaker system consisted of only four songs: "Paper Roses" by Marie Osmond, "Build Me Up, Buttercup," "Soldier Boy," and one other song I have mercifully forgotten. This panoply of musical goodness was piped into our eager ears from four scratchy 45s playing on a tiny record player set up halfway around the far side of the rink in a small room that also contained a life-sized plastic reindeer and a chair. Why we never questioned this arrangement of objects still baffles me.

Ma Long left her post at the front desk and shuffled onto the rink, around the outside edge (to avoid getting whacked by overly enthusiastic ten-year-olds), and over to the record player to put the four 45s back up onto the spindle after the last one was done playing. And, at her rate of speed—wearing her wrinkled apron, three layers of cotton skirts, stockings, leggings, an old button-down sweater, and a pair of slippers that must have been family heirlooms by now—well, she barely made it back to the front desk before she had to turn around and shuffle back to the record player to pull the four songs back up onto the spindle again. I think the chair was over there for her to rest and catch her breath before starting back. I still have no idea what the plastic reindeer was for.

This wasn't the oddest part of the skating rink. The crowning achievement of this rink's design was its bathrooms. Someone in his infinite wisdom designed this rink with the bathrooms accessible only from the skating floor itself. So, if you were sitting in the ante-room still lacing up your skates halfway into the party and found you had to relieve yourself, you still had to skate your way onto the rink (no street shoes allowed on the rink floor!), into traffic, and whirr about 345 de-grees around the rink counterclockwise before hitting the bathroom door. And, I do mean "hitting" the bath-room door because, in another brilliant architectural move, the bathroom doors swung *outward* onto the rink floor. Any child who had attended more than one party knew not to skate anywhere near those doors, for fear of getting slammed in the face. Which, by the way, happened frequently.

Those fortunate enough to make it to the door without getting a concussion had to grab the handle with both hands to keep from sailing right past the bathroom. This usually meant you'd end up hanging onto that door handle for dear life, with your legs hav-ing given out under you, your butt just inches from the floor. Once you got yourself upright again, it was no easy feat to get the door open while on wheels. And, what awaited you once you got the door open was a treat beyond imagination: *The bathroom floor went down-hill at a twenty-degree angle.*

Picture, if you can, uncoordinated ten-year-olds let-ting go of that door handle and careening downhill on skates—improperly laced—toward the far wall at the bottom. *Smack!* The trick then was to grab the handles of each toilet stall and pull yourself back uphill to the first available stall.

You've never truly lived until you've used a toilet on roller skates at a twenty-degree sideways incline. You always ended up leaning into the downward wall of the stall while trying to be as delicate as possible going about your business. They should have made it an Olympic sport. It would have given a whole new meaning to the phrase "Going for the Gold!"

Once you found a way to get straightened back up and out of the stall, you somehow had to skate across the downward grade to the sinks. Putting four porcelain sinks in a downhill bathroom used by young girls on wheels was a stroke of marketing genius. How this place got insurance is beyond me. You had to grab one faucet to hang on and wash your hands with the other without accidentally turning your feet anywhere near the downward angle of the floor. I don't know how many lives must have been lost when girls tried to clutch at the metal faucets or porcelain sinks on their way back down the incline of the bathroom floor.

And, of course, once you were done washing your hands, the worst part of the escapade awaited you: the long, desperate climb up the floor and back out of the bathroom. Clutching the faucets of the four sinks carried you only so far, and then you were left with about five or six feet of bare uphill floor and no more handles before you made it back to the door. Some brave souls clung to the wainscoting with their outstretched palms, but I was too afraid to attempt something so futile and risky. I always dropped to my hands and knees and *crawled* up to the door, grabbing the inside door handle and pulling myself up. And I have a funny feeling those floors didn't get mopped all that often, so there went the whole concept of washing your hands.

The last part of the adventure was trying to open the door without killing someone. (Remember: The door opened outward onto the rink.) Most of us opened the door slowly . . . *carefully* . . . sliding out sideways without opening the door very far and hoping we didn't get bombarded by oncoming skaters. Did I mention we were on wheels?

After an hour of this fun and frivolity, it was time to have the mid-party birthday cake and soda! All thirty of us headed for the anteroom and sat on the rickety bench chairs lining the wall, waiting for Ma Long's assistant to shuffle past us in her own deteriorating slippers, asking us each what kind of soda we wanted. This assistant was rumored to be a woman, although she had the gravelly voice of a chain-smoker and wore a skirt and pants at the same time, along with a moth-eaten sweater or two. Or three. I don't know why she bothered to ask what flavor we wanted because we all eagerly yelled, "Chocolate!" There's nothing less nutritious and tasty than an old, cheap, generic chocolate soda that hasn't been properly refrigerated, but we didn't care. We never got this stuff at home.

Once we were stuffed with birthday cake and chocolate soda that had separated like oil and water, we headed back out to the rink for the second hour of the party. We avoided the show-off who could skate backwards and brought her own skates (with actual laces and those rubber stoppers in the front). We avoided skating anywhere near the bathroom doors. We went by the record player and the plastic reindeer and waved, secretly hoping the thing would wink or move. We veered away from Ma Long as she shuffled past us to change the records. And, if she was feeling as frisky as an eighty-year-old again, she might turn on the disco ball that hung at center rink and shout into the scratchy microphone, *"Turn around and skate the other way!"* The combination of the flashing disco ball and the sudden change in orientation made us confused and a little nauseous. There's nothing safer than thirty queasy schoolkids on roller skates in a dark room with blinking lights.

Ma Long passed away many years ago, and I don't know if the rink is still standing. Perhaps safety violations have caught up with it over the years as humorless parents decided you shouldn't have to climb out of a bathroom on wheels or risk getting hit with a flying door. But I'm betting there's still a case of that chocolate soda in the back room somewhere. Dust it off and pass me one, would you, for old time's sake?   ❖

Who You Callin' Chicken?

There's nothing quite like teaching one's firstborn the subtleties and complexities of the English language. Nothing compares to the joy and thrill of first-time parents as they watch their adorable fledgling rise from the oceans of speechless, grunting communication and soar to the heights of deep, meaningful interaction.

And then there's what happened to us.

Christopher, our firstborn, who had been ahead of his peers in nearly all stages of his development, except perhaps learning to operate anything mechanical (a peculiarity that continues to this day), had started noticing correlations between words and the delicate interplay of parts of speech. I know he wouldn't have put it like that at the time (well, probably not), but he truly was verbally gifted (or, as his grandmother would say, "Verbally gifted? Is that what we're calling it now? In my day we just called it talkative"). Once, when his younger brother, Jeremy, was asked why he himself never spoke, he said, "God gave Christopher a lot to say, and He gave me a lot to do." Truer words were never spoken.

So, in these earlier days, we beamed with pride one night at dinner as linguistic genius Christopher sat in his booster seat and munched on his potatoes and roast chicken.

"Isn't it funny how there's an animal called 'chicken' and a food called 'chicken' too?"

We nodded approvingly, smiles widening.

"Yes, Christopher. They're the same thing."

"What do you mean they're the same thing?"

Still smiling, pleased that he was learning a fascinating new language concept, the explanation continued.

"Well, the food chicken that you're eating came from the animal chicken on a farm."

We could almost hear the cogs and wheels turning in his big-boy brain as this notion slowly worked its way into his awareness. I mentally counted off the seconds waiting for the proverbial light bulb to go off over his head. Instead, the inquisitive look on his face morphed into one of horror. He looked down at his plate and dropped the fork, letting it clank to the floor. And then, with a wailing reminiscent of someone cataloguing the fall of the Hindenburg, he howled with grief.

"Oh no! The poor chickens! All the poor chickens!" Stunned into silence, we looked at each other and then back at Christopher, who was weeping and covering his face in anguish. We knew he was a sensitive child, but honestly—it was just a chicken.

"Christopher, it's okay, really. The chicken—"

But Christopher had already had another change of facial expression. He was now sniffling and collecting himself, sitting up straighter, and pushed his plate away from him.

"That's it!" he declared, with the determined voice of someone vowing to go forth and sin no more. "I'll never eat chicken again!" He crossed his hands over his chest and looked at us blankly.

My first thought was, "Hey, disaster averted." My second thought was, "Now what do I cook? He can't eat peanut butter and jelly for dinner."

But, before I had time to mull over possible solutions to the culinary dilemma created by my darling son, he'd solved the problem for us, announcing with the pride of the naive and inexperienced:

"I'll just have a hamburger instead."

We looked at each other across the table. *Should we? No, not today.*   ♣

Medieval Instruments of Torture in My Hallway

I was driving home from work today—well, driving to the Barnes & Noble, really, since I had a ton of writing to do—and I started to think about stray objects I have in my house, especially the things that have no discernibly logical purpose. My mind immediately leapt to the crossbow sitting in the hallway near our downstairs bathroom.

Yes, dear reader, I have a crossbow in my hallway. Yes, one of those zany weapons that looks like the bastard lovechild of a bow-and-arrow and a rifle. It's currently in its original cardboard box, properly labeled with a color picture and the word "crossbow" and all that stuff, and the whole box is leaning up against an unused treadmill. Where else would it be? The slogan under the photo of a man with the crossbow is: "The

Adventure Starts Here." Well, the adventure might start in the *woods*, or the *gamelands* in the neighboring county, but I assure you the adventure doesn't start here. Not in my hallway next to a treadmill.

I'm still not entirely clear why this medieval apparatus is leaning against the treadmill in the hallway, but it's been there for a while. When I stumble bleary-eyed to the bathroom in the middle of the night, I walk right by this torture-machine as if it were the most natural thing in the world. Do all my friends have to endure things like this? Perhaps other women meander past guillotines in bubble wrap at two A.M., or saunter by wooden catapults in Tyvek envelopes near dawn . . . but I walk past a crossbow in a cardboard box, because the adventure starts here.

One of these nights I'm going to accidentally bump into the box, setting off the crossbow and having to explain to my husband the next morning why there is a T-shaped hole in the hallway ceiling.

He should understand, though. He's the one who put it there in the first place.

Not that any of you were surprised to hear that. ✤

Open 23 Hours

I was driving on Route 65, minding my own business, which isn't difficult to do in a nondescript Ford from the 1980s. No one's paying attention to me anyway, except when they're right up my back bumper, cursing at me in nasty little snippets of foul language and then passing me in a huff as soon as that port authority bus gets out of the way.

At a traffic light in Ambridge, I looked left at the line of cross traffic waiting for its green light to click in. At the front of the line sat a tow truck—nothing attached to its hitch—with this painted on the side: "23-Hr. Towing."

I had a few minutes to stare at this slogan while the truck waited for the green light. I wondered what the guy did with that last remaining hour in the day.

Did he grab a quick catnap during Hour 24, so he'd be only a *little* bug-eyed and lethargic when Hour 1 rolled around again? Also, which hour didn't he tow things? Was it the same hour every day? How did he decide which hour not to tow things? Was there a particular hour in the day that was already light on tow-truck demands? I could only assume that perhaps he took his nap from, like, three A.M. to four A.M. I thought perhaps folks needed a tow truck mighty rarely during that particular hour of the night.

Then again, if someone needed a tow truck between the hours of three and four in the morning, they probably *really* needed that tow truck. Would our tow-truck driver be losing a lot of revenue in grateful tips and added late-night fees by not towing things between three o'clock and four o'clock? This suddenly wasn't as simple as it initially appeared.

I struggled to comprehend what would make a small tow-truck company paint something as perplexing and epistemologically curious as "23-Hr. Towing" on the side of its truck. Was it a typo? Hard to fathom someone accidentally painting the wrong number of hours in the day on the side of a truck—on both sides—in big white letters, and not noticing the error before taking the vehicle out on the road. Although the paint job looked fairly new, it didn't look *that* new. The guy had been driving around with this inexplicable slogan for a while now. It apparently meant something to other people. It just didn't mean anything to me.

I wasn't sure I'd ever get up the courage to call these

people if I needed my car towed. I'm just self-esteem-less enough to know deep down that the very hour my car breaks down is the one hour in the day that this guy isn't towing things. Plus, I'm the queen of worst-case scenarios.

I'd love an excuse to call these people to find out just what "23-Hr. Towing" means, but I'd probably chicken out. We have a AAA membership and free towing is included, probably even between the hours of three and four A.M. Along with being a worst-case scenario person, I'm also cheap.

And, in my world of thrift stores and coupons and Walmart, cheap beats curious every time. So, the mystery remains.   ❖

There's An Echo in Here

I'm sitting here in the comfort of my own home, upstairs in My New Office®, typing on a nice computer hooked up to the Internet via cable modem, listening to iTunes, drinking coffee brewed right here in My New Office®, with creamer I got from the dorm fridge behind me on the countertop in My New Office®. Can you tell I just upgraded my entire home office?

It's raining outside and getting a little dark already, and I'm cozy and warm and totally non-bored here inside the house, with too many choices of what to do.

And, what are my parents doing? They're sitting in an empty house about fifteen minutes from here, with little more than two fold-up camping chairs, a couple of cardboard boxes as end tables, a lamp on the floor, a cooler in the kitchen, and an air mattress in the bedroom.

Now, they could be doing this because they are essentially boring, dull people with absolutely no sense of adventure or hobbies. But that's not entirely true. They're really sitting there all alone because:

1. I have work to do here (an article to write and a song parody to compose), although obviously I'm not doing that work at the moment.

2. They're stubborn and they realize we'd all drive each other nuts if we were in the same house on a rainy day for too long. (Think *Cat in the Hat*.)

3. They're waiting for the moving company truck to show up with all their stuff.

If you chose number 4 (all of the above, *not pictured*), you're absolutely right.

Apparently my parents moved all the way from Las Vegas to Beaver County, Pennsylvania, but their stuff decided to make a detour through Maryland first and may not be here until Saturday. This fits perfectly with my mother's ongoing battle cry of "What's our last name again?"

There is evidently some sort of family curse based on the two letters of our last name that accounts for every "Murphy's Law" type of occurrence in our lives (although our name isn't Murphy, so I don't quite get the connection but my mother does and that's ultimately what matters when in this type of situation and by the way where was I?).

I have experienced this curse firsthand and so know it to be empirically verifiable fact; however, I also know that I personally liked being an Au for the twenty-five years I was one legally (twenty before my first marriage and five between the first marriage and this one). So, either I so thoroughly enjoyed being an Au that it offset the family curse, or the curse's targets just aren't big enough things to dwell on.

This, from someone who dwells on everything. Yeah.

So, with all this belly-button lint collecting on our mutual contemplation of the situation, my parents sit in an empty house in the rain, and I sit here writing about their wretched existence fifteen minutes away from me. Something dreadfully weird and unfair about that, but not enough to get up and go over there for.

After all, they have the cable and Internet guy scheduled to come tomorrow—but the TV and computer are somewhere in Maryland.

They have a toaster oven, microwave and coffeemaker, but no refrigerator. My dad was outside pulling up fencing around their back porch, getting grimy and dirty—but they have no washer or dryer yet.

Joker (their weird dog-like cat) is bored to tears and keeps trying to find a comfortable spot on someone's lap in the camping chairs, which just ain't hap'nin'. He stares out the windows and wonders where all the cactuses went that used to be out there. Indoor cats are really easy to confound.

My parents' new hobby until their stuff shows up seems to be driving around looking for Bush/Cheney signs (so they know which neighbors to borrow things from) or going to Walmart to buy brooms or window-shopping at the local hardware store for kitchen cabi-net handles.

Really, their lives sound infinitely more interesting than mine at the moment, which consists of gulping down coffee, listening to Linkin Park and Frou Frou, and staring at the article specs for an upcoming Chicken Soup book I hope to contribute to.

Did I mention it's raining?

I'm starting to think my parents' stuff—wherever it is—is having more fun than I am. At least it's off some-where seeing the world.   ♣

People . . . People Who Watch People

I like watching people, and the way I do it, it's technically not stalking. I do this a lot, even while I'm driving the stupid little half-rusty Ford Escort home from work and I should be watching the road a little more closely because I'm in the smallest, least trustworthy car on the road. Statistically, it's in my best interests.

Today I spotted a man walking from one parking lot to another in a small shopping center along Route 65. He must have been around fifty, perhaps a little older. He was dressed in this odd assortment of clothes that made absolutely no fashion statement at all. I didn't think that was even possible until I saw this man today. I mean, everyone's wardrobe makes some sort of statement about them, even if it's "I'm a total dweeb," or "I couldn't match my clothes properly even if they were on matching Garanimals hangers in my closet," or perhaps "I don't look like the kind of person you want to get too close to without a can of Mace."

But this guy was making no statement at all. I couldn't figure out how he dressed himself. Oddly, all his clothing looked clean, so I didn't get a sense of thriftstoreitis about him. But nothing made sense. He was wearing rather white (okay, glowing) sneakers, the kind worn by someone who normally participates in athletic activity at least once a year. But he didn't look like he'd participated in so much as a chess match in the park with the old guys on Tuesday afternoons.

Above the sneakers he wore a crisply pressed pair of gray Dockers, but with too much pleating in the front to suit him well. Plus, with the sneakers, the overly neat Dockers just looked, well, out of place.

Above that was a silvery, shiny zip-up jacket. It had that eighties tacky look that made me think back to the bad ol' days. (There weren't many good ol' days for most people, fashion-wise, in the eighties.)

Under the silvery, tacky/shiny jacket was a red T-shirt with some sort of writing on it. Just a regular-looking red T-shirt. A little bit wrinkly, in fact. And the writing on the shirt was worn, as if perhaps it was a favorite shirt worn and washed so often that it showed its age and then some.

He was carrying a paper bag sideways under one arm and something that could have been a large car part under the other. I don't know why. He didn't look like he was walking to his car. He was out near the road, just walking. Who buys car parts (large ones, at that) for cars they don't have, or, at least, don't have with them?

To top off the look (or lack of it), he wore a red baseball cap on his head—backwards. Now, I'm sorry, but no one over twelve should wear a baseball hat backwards anymore, and certainly no one who's not into hip-hop. This guy was instantly disqualified on both counts.

And yet there sat the ball cap on his head—backwards. Defiantly backwards. And yet he didn't even know he was defying anything. I could tell. He just put the hat on that way.

While sitting at the light staring at this guy, I fleetingly thought perhaps he had a story. I'm a writer; I should be able to figure out this guy's story, or make one up.

Just as I was contemplating the possibility of his alter ego being L.L. Cool Walter or something, the Alpha Romeo Spider behind me beeped. The light had turned green. I hate when that happens.

I've been home from work for two hours and I still haven't figured this guy out. Do I lack imagination, or does this man defy description because he fits into absolutely no category? He's probably just as boring as he looks. But I hope not.

In closing, in my own defense as an avowed people-watcher, let me offer a chart of differences between a people-watcher and a stalker, in case you find yourself in a people-watching situation:

PEOPLE-WATCHING	STALKING
It's an innocent activity.	Not so much, really . . .
You're curious about all people equally.	You're focused on one person, often someone smarter and better-looking than you.
You stay in one place, happy to watch people pass.	You follow one person around, hiding in bushes.
You take cute, humorous notes in a little black notebook so you don't forget wacky things you see.	You take copious notes in tiny, tight handwriting, collecting it in 27 scrapbooks you keep under a floorboard in your closet.
You chuckle cheerily at the funny things people around you are doing.	You drool over what you're seeing in someone's bedroom window with those night-vision goggles.
You search through the trash bin in the park after you see a child accidentally drop in a favorite toy while throwing away her candy wrapper.	You root through the garbage at someone's house, looking for old gas station receipts, coffee grounds, and bits of rancid food the person might have touched so you can frame it and hang it on a secret wall in your basement.
No one who's watching you watching others will call the police on you.	Two words: *restraining order*

More Random Things
I Notice

List #2: Important Stuff to Remember:

• Never try to jury-rig a WiFi connection with a wire coat hanger and chewing gum connected to your laptop with a twist-tie from an old bread bag, no matter what my husband tells you. It won't work. He was just filching off the neighbor's unsecure network and didn't know it. (This is not to be confused with an "insecure network," which is just a fancy, high-tech-sounding name for my group of women friends when we get together for dinner.)

• Never pray for patience.

• I opened a bag of corn chips today and noticed a small logo in the lower right corner of the bag: "Official Snack of Minor League Baseball." Take note of that:

Minor League. Somehow this bag of yummy snack food didn't make it to the Show. What does this say about the chips?

• Ever notice that clichés regarding work involve torture-chamber levels of pain? Putting your nose to the grindstone. Working your fingers to the bone. It's a good thing we don't realize as kids that this stuff is far closer to literal than any of us want to admit. We'd have thrown ourselves off bridges the first chance we got.

• I don't care how fast you want it: Never, *ever* pray for patience.

• During one week, I see a news story about a study saying that coffee is good for you. The next week, a new study asserts that coffee is bad for you. So, just to be safe, I drink coffee every other week.

• There's something about Velveeta that creeps me out a little bit. My husband may have grown up with the stuff and may indeed have fond memories of eating it as a child, but anything called "processed cheese food product" that can also be branded with a half-life just shouldn't be ingested.

• I'm serious: *Don't pray for patience.* It's a trick. ✤

Stuff in My Car That Doesn't Work

It's been another of those muggy weeks here in western Pennsylvania where I become a hermit in my house, enjoying the constant 74 degrees and low humidity of our central air. I turn into a wuss unable to leave the house to do anything unnecessary. Doesn't help that the air conditioning in my car doesn't really do much more than cool off my knees and my right elbow because the only cold air I feel seeps out of the vents and only the body parts in a three-inch radius from a vent get cooled off. And frankly, driving with my face hunched down in front of a side vent really wouldn't do much for my driving record. Not really.

Where was I? Oh yeah.

We're moving a big bookcase into the house from our storage facility, so I may get the rest of my books in here, and also the rest of my vinyl record albums. Yes, kids, you don't remember such things, but we old fogeys played vinyl record albums instead of CDs.

It's a weird thought that none of my now-grown children know how to operate a turntable. I'm not saying I miss vinyl, despite the many things I've read about how compromised CD sound is compared to vinyl. I certainly don't miss playing songs in a different order by lifting up the needle at the end of one song and physically placing it on the beginning of the song you want to hear next (which may have entailed flipping over the album first and holding in that little metal thingy at the top of the spindle so the album would fall all the way down and sit flat on the turntable). And I certainly don't miss hearing that scraping sound of a needle scoring its way across the album, leaving a nice scratch in its wake that usually meant hearing a skip at that precise point in the song every time you played it from then on.

And none of us would have been able to play vinyl albums in our cars like we can with CDs and now iPods. Can you picture trying to shove a big ol' twelve-inch album into a huge slot in your dashboard, which would have taken up the entire width of the car? Instead, we'd all still be stuck playing cassettes in the car, hitting FF or REW in a vain attempt to skip songs on albums we hate without causing traffic accidents.

Then again, in my case, even that would be a step up. Over a year ago my husband got me a CD player for my car. (I'm driving a '92 Corsica, made before technology was invented.) I was thrilled to replace my tape deck, and except for the fact that it apparently had no skip protection whatsoever, especially for burned CDs ("Don't breathe, Jeremy, or it'll skip over every three seconds of your favorite Good Charlotte song"), I was thrilled to have this technology available in my car.

For approximately six months.

Then the contraption woke up one morning and decided to forget what a CD looked like. And it hasn't recognized a CD since. We've tried every type of CD in the book. We tried every type of cleaner known to mankind (except peanut butter, which every preschooler seems to think belongs in CD players). Nothing worked. Certainly not the CDs. So then I was reduced to using it as a very, very bad radio. Which was worse than the radio that had been in my tape deck.

Then the thing started to physically slip out of the slot in the dashboard. When I drove up a hill, the whole CD player (or, should I say, "the very expensive yet *cheap* radio"?) would slide out the rectangular hole and whack the gear shift. I had to drive with one hand holding the thing in place to keep it from ramming the car into neutral, which got dangerous after a while.

I asked my husband to disconnect the CD player entirely, and all I had left staring at me from the hole in the dash were about two dozen wires of different colors. Oh sure, they were pretty, but . . .

Someday I hope to get him to put the tape deck back in. I'm actually looking forward to the day when I'll be able to play a *tape* in my *car* again. My standards have gotten really low in the past six months.

Till then I have no CD player, no tape deck, no radio, and no clock in my car. Nada. Zip. Zilch. Total silence when I drive. Well, except for when my kids are in the car. There's never total silence then, of course.

But, it'll be months till I see another radio or tape deck in my car. Why? Because my husband would have to sit in my cramped, sweltering car jiggling wires around for hours on end. And, of course, it's August.

Oh well. Maybe for Christmas. . . . Oh wait, it'll be snowing then. He won't want to sit outside in my car then either.

What's the old saying? Silence is golden? I wish I could agree.   ♣

Back Me Up

Today I'm in pain. I must've moved the wrong way or turned funny or coughed or something (also known as exercising at my age). The muscles along the right side of my back went haywire and since then it's been torture to move—but only in certain directions. Like, to the right. Or the left. I have trouble sitting, getting back up, twisting to one side, reaching down with my right arm, and a whole host of other mundane gerundial movements. I'm sitting in a chair right now dreading hoisting myself up. More than usual, I mean.

The obvious explanation for my dilemma is that I shouldn't have dragged that five-shelf bookcase up a flight of stairs to the second floor this morning. It's obvious now, but it seemed like a good idea at the time. And, really, I didn't do anything extraordinary. I just eased the thing up onto each step, one at a time. I don't recall pulling any muscles then, and the pain didn't come till hours later, after I'd been sitting on the couch for a few hours doing a lot of nothing. You know, a typical evening at my house. Still, the mind wants to make connections, and this is the easiest explanation that accounts for the data.

But, it could have happened while I was vacuuming the entryway. (That'll teach me to clean the house.) At one point the belt slipped off the upright vacuum and I had to un-upright it and take the plastic bottom off, holding the whole contraption between my knees at a weird angle and cleaning out the gunk and hair while putting the belt back on properly. Perhaps I held something at an odd angle for too long and yanked something then. Besides the vacuum belt, I mean.

Doesn't matter. I'd love to sink into the waterbed right now and let the heated water in the mattress help the muscles unknot. But I'm afraid I won't be able to get back out and I'd be declared lost at sea. (See "Water, Water Everywhere" on page 95.)

Plus, the TV that was in our bedroom had to be sent back to the cable company (we got it free as part of their cable rewards program so we got what we paid for), so we're TV-less in that room for the next few weeks.

This would be a perfect time to read a book, but I've never quite mastered the art of reading a book in that sloshy waterbed. Severe seasickness comes to mind. *My* mind. Literally.

Oh, dear. I feel my entire right side tensing up

again. A hot shower earlier had loosened things up enough to move around with only a little excruciating, searing pain—which was an improvement—but the effects seem to be wearing off. I can't turn to the right at all now.

As a last resort I may climb into Wayne's recliner with a book and the TV remote. Sounds like nirvana for a lot of people, but it's tough for me to get comfortable in that thing. It's made for people well over six feet tall, not short things topping out at five feet, two inches. I feel like Edith Ann in her rocking chair, legs dangling six inches off the floor.

But lying in the recliner would give me the support I need for my back and the creature comforts I'm not ready to do without right now.

I may resort to getting the hot water bottle, which is only for very old people who actually know how to use them without scalding their asses.

It's not a bad idea, really, to try that—or anything else—as long as I don't have to turn to the right to do it.   ✤

Field Trip to the Drive-In

Last night the kids and I had the brilliant idea to go to the drive-in to see a double-header of *Finding Nemo* and *Tomb Raider 2*. We spent the early evening scrambling around getting ready. I popped some popcorn, the girls helped pack up the car with a blanket, four camping chairs, and a cooler (with grapes, cauliflower—Grace's favorite munchie on the Atkins diet—and some ranch dressing to dip the cauliflower in). We scurried out of here a few minutes later than I would have liked, but we didn't forget to bring anything.

Or so we thought.

We stopped at a local beverage place to get cans of soda ("pop" in western Pennsylvania, but I refuse to call it "pop," ever) and were finally off. Made it through the construction on Route 60 and were soon outside the drive-in waiting in line to turn in off the street and get into the driveway of the theater. An employee was doing a walk-through telling everyone that *American Wedding* was sold out, which didn't bother us, of course. In fact, all the cars turning around and leaving ahead of us made getting off the street that much easier. We paid our cheap fees to get in and the ticket window worker told us to make sure to tune our radios to 97.5 FM to get the sound for our movie. (Each screen has its own radio frequency—a far cry from the days when we used to grab a big metal contraption off a metal stand at our parking spots and hook it onto the car window and had to make a mental note not to leave with the thing still stuck to the window.)

I'm sure you all know where this is going by now. But I digress.

The place was so crowded we ended up making our own parking spot, way down front, way off to the right (almost up against the guard rail over the road below). I made sure all the windows were down before turning off the car. And, I instinctively reached for the radio dial to turn it to *97.5 . . . F . . . M . . .*

There was only a hole—and some loose wires— *where my radio used to be.* I forgot Wayne had taken out the faulty tape deck.

Somehow, the now-obvious fact that we should have brought a boombox with batteries had totally escaped me while I was popping popcorn and buying cans of soda (not pop) and generally running around like an idiot a few hours earlier.

After a collective smacking of foreheads, we decided to steal everyone else's radio noise by setting up our camping chairs by the car with the loudest radio. We set up the chairs close enough to hear their radio but not so close that we'd have to marry anyone in the morning. Worked quite well for *Finding Nemo*. Had no trouble hearing anything. That was the up side of having the place full of cars. Radios everywhere.

But, as usually happens with drive-ins playing two flicks, a nice handful of people (the ones with little kids who came mainly for *Finding Nemo,* which was pretty much everybody within a two-mile radius) left at the intermission. Once *Tomb Raider 2* came on we had trouble finding a spot close enough to hear someone else's radio. Not without being so blatantly obvious that they'd call the authorities. And once Addie ended up in the back seat of the car half-asleep, we called it a night and came home—about a half-hour into *Tomb Raider*.

For those of you not familiar with drive-ins and drive-in etiquette: Don't get the impression that we just chummed up to strangers. Well, we did—a little. But most everyone brings camping chairs, mosquito candles, coolers, and blankets and sits outside their cars. I just love the atmosphere of the drive-in.

But I also love *hearing* a movie I've paid to see, so it was best to leave early and learn our lesson. (*Note to Self:* Beg husband to reinstall tape deck.)

It's been a long weekend.   ❖

The Winter of Their Discontent

My folks have been living here in western Pennsylvania for a little while now. They grew up on the eastern side of the state and raised my brother and me there, then retired ten years early and moved to Las Vegas to gamble away our inheritance. You know, like most parents do.

But, after a decade of living the high life, they moved back east to be closer to the grandchildren. However, until they moved here, I'd never lived closer to my parents than three hundred miles. Having them five miles away is very, very different.

So far, it's worked out well. They know not to stop by my house any time before ten A.M. or they will be shot on sight, and I know not to call their house any time after nine P.M. because they probably went to bed as soon as it got dark. Once we got the night owl/morning person thing cleared up, everything else seemed to fall into place. And I find I'm truly enjoying having them in the same county with me.

At dinner, my mother and I can discuss the beauty and wonder of Pennsylvania potholes, a phenomenon she and my father had all but forgotten out west in Nevada. She will quickly relearn that, in Pennsylvania, people exchange pothole stories the way some men swap fishing or golf stories. ("Oh yeah? My PT Cruiser fell into a pothole the size of Aunt Martha's butt!")

I predict it'll all come back to them in a post-traumatic-stress-disorder sort of way sometime in mid-February. Then there will be weeping and gnashing of teeth. And tires. Gnashing of tires too. That's the really ugly part.

And, it's fun to hear these Las Vegas folks say things like, "Gee, it's cold!" fifty times in one visit. In June.

Then again, my dad is the same guy who, when he moved to Vegas in 1994, kept saying things like, "Gee, it's so *hot!*" And my mother kept saying, "Yes, John, you live in a desert, remember?" How this slipped his mind is beyond me. They had an eight-foot cactus in their front yard.

So, now, when she says it's cold (while wearing twelve layers of thermal clothing), I just shake my head and roll my eyes.

Then again, I have a husband who spends most of the winter going barefoot around our house, wearing shorts and T-shirts, and turning the heat up to 74 degrees. The logic of this escapes me. Apparently he didn't know that you're not supposed to turn up the heat back east—you're supposed to add another eleven layers of clothing, ear muffs, and big, fuzzy slippers. And brew another pot of decaf.

He could take some lessons from my mother on how to keep warm. She's an expert. Just not in Pennsylvania.   ❖

Eat'n Puke

One of the perks of living in western Pennsylvania — besides the great baseball team and more annual rainfall than Seattle — is a chain of family restaurants called Eat'n Park. Charming, inexpensive, clean, and low-key enough to tolerate families with toddlers, it quickly became a favorite place to eat out when the children were very little.

So, when I found myself spending my first Valentine's Day post-divorce with a three-year-old and a one-year-old in tow, the logical thing to do was to pick myself up, dust myself off, and take the three of us out to our local Eat'n Park for dinner. After all, the girls were too young to understand the poignant nature of the occasion, and it felt good to take my mind off what had become the lousiest holiday of the year (with the possible exception of National Eggs Benedict Day on April 16).

As we ate, my one-year-old daughter, Addie, merely sucked on whatever bits of food I gave her from my own plate but Grace, the three-year-old, chose her own dinner of chicken fingers and fries, both of which she promptly slathered with ketchup. (Heinz, of course— it's required by law in western Pennsylvania.)

The evening might have turned out better if I had gone with my instincts and said no to her request for chocolate milk to accompany her chicken and fries. (To be blunt, the evening would have turned out better if I had stayed home, locked myself in a closet with a rabid weasel, and fed us both cold sauerkraut through a straw, but hindsight is 20/20.) And perhaps I still had a chance of salvaging the experience if I had said no to her request for a second glass of chocolate milk. Or said no to her insisting that she gulp it down as if she were part of a pit crew gassing up Jeff Gordon's car. And oh, the things that might have been different if I had factored in her congenital motion sickness and easily upset stomach . . .

But no, I was feeling indulgent as only an eternally guilt-ridden mother can feel, and I allowed Grace all these personal excesses because the glee on her little toddler face seemed worth it—at the time.

At the end of our meal, I stood and lifted baby Addie out of the high chair, slinging her onto my hip. I motioned to Grace to stand and get ready to leave. She hoisted back her glass for that last chug of chocolate milk before standing on the bench seat for all around us to see. She was so darned adorable standing there smiling at the admiring groups of little old ladies who were seated in neighboring booths, all of us celebrating this Valentine's Day bereft of male companionship but yet happy to be with friends and family. She soaked up the murmured compliments and smiles, and so did I as the proud mother.

Until Grace said, softly but urgently, "Uh oh."

I had just enough time to look at her, standing on that seat, now at eye level with me, before it hit me that a social disaster of epic proportions was about to occur.

And yet, instead I asked, "What's wrong, Grace?"

"I think I'm going to be—"

That last word, which was painfully unnecessary by this time, was cut off by a thick brown volcanic eruption that emanated from her tiny little mouth, arcing upward in a vaulted stream and then down to the table below with the force of Old Faithful and a curvature that fleetingly reminded me of the St. Louis Arch. Bits of chicken breading took a road less traveled, landing at other points in the booth and tempting me to yell out "Fire in the hole!" for everyone's safety.

Instead, I stood rooted silently to the floor, watching as Grace's projectile vomiting continued with no hope of ever letting up. The look on Grace's face had changed from the previous moment's sanguine smile to abject horror at the shock she was imposing on everyone around us. In that instant, I again knew what was coming next but was oddly paralyzed to stop it.

The slow-motion camera that activates whenever tragic phenomena occur had just kicked in, and I watched in dismay as Grace—with the knowledge of basic physics of a three-year-old—tried to obstruct the forward progress of the vomit-volcano by placing her hands in front of her still-spewing mouth.

Unfortunately, the hands of a three-year-old are tiny and unable to block the unstoppable force that is projectile vomiting. Much as a poorly built dam will eventually burst, allowing the water to flow unimpeded in any direction it wishes, so too was the reappearance of Grace's dinner. As she desperately continued to clamp both her hands over her mouth, the unrelenting puke-stream merely found its easiest point of opening: between her fingers.

All this did was redirect the chocolate gush straight upward, covering her face, soaking even her eyelashes on its way across the top of her head and into every corner of her otherwise gorgeous, glossy black hair. I began to question my own recollection of the laws of physics as I watched in repulsed fascination the strange gravity-defying path of the chunk-laden stream before me.

Perhaps only five seconds had passed since the first eruption. Yet, of course, it seemed more like endless purgatorial hours of torture, watching this continue and only staring from afar. Little Addie continued to cling to my left hip, oblivious to the detritus (and globs of ketchup) now coagulating all over the booth table and seats. But, naturally, the incident hadn't escaped the notice of several Eat'n Park employees, and a handful of nearby patrons, who were likely vowing next time to stick to the nursing home dinner buffet, which never served chocolate milk for this very reason. I slowly became aware of the service people around us, several of whom had rushed up with large terrycloth towels, which they flung onto the table in a frantic attempt to cover up the offensive bits and pieces of, well, whatever this stuff had been before this uncontrolled toddler had gotten a hold of it.

I heard myself apologizing in a stunned monotone that smacked of clinical shock, sounding muffled and far away, part of that same slow-motion effect that hadn't left since the first molecules of chocolate resurfaced nearly a minute earlier. No one was listening to me, though. Total situational anarchy had broken out, with mops and muffled screaming now added to the towels in the ongoing vain effort to stanch the hemorrhage of reemergent dinner items swimming in a chocolate geyser.

Then, as suddenly as it began, the surging swell of supper ended. As the employees rushed around mopping and toweling, while mumbling incoherent but likely imprecatory turns of phrase, Addie yawned on my hip, and I held my breath waiting for Round Two. Grace cautiously moved her useless toddler hands away from her mouth, blinking chocolate drops off her long black eyelashes and looking at me for guidance.

None was forthcoming. I was busy planning our escape route. The townspeople were restless. ♣

Cinderella Understood Writers

Because writing does not yet pay the bills for me, it too often remains at the bottom of my to-do list each day. I've heard all the suggestions about carving out time for writing, about making it such a priority that you hang a sign on your home office door that says, "Don't bother me unless you're bleeding or something is on fire. I'm writing!"

As things are going currently, there are a few things wrong with these suggestions at my house. First, my home office has no door. The house used to be apartments, and my office used to be the upstairs kitchen. There was a bifold door on it when my son used it as a bedroom (the only bedroom with a sink and cabinets), but that's now buried somewhere up in the attic. Trust me: No one wants to venture up there to look for a bifold door just so I can hang a paper sign on it.

Another dilemma is that I was blessed at birth with an innate sense of panic, anxiety and guilt. If someone in the house is upset, it is automatically my fault and I must make things right. If someone feels bored, I must entertain the masses. If someone needs a load of laundry done, I must drop what I am doing and take the laundry basket down to the basement. Despite being a mediocre cook, and despite having a semi-empty nest, I am also responsible for dinner, and in some cases lunch. I pack lunches for family members who work outside the house. I also do grocery shopping, clutter-control, and the modest amount of cleaning I can bring myself to endure.

And, of course, I do freelance copy editing, proofreading, and sometimes typesetting as projects come in. I rarely turn down projects—part of that "Just Say Yes" syndrome that we guilt-ridden folks are born with. We don't wish to hurt anyone's feelings, even clients we've met only through e-mails, and so we say yes to everything and then hope a calendar day magically becomes forty hours long.

In my guilt-ridden mind, all of these things must come before writing. I pick up on the unspoken opinion that the writing should come in dead last, after I take out your trash or paint your living room or run to the bank or take you to the movies or a trip to the store for some Very Important Personal Shopping at the last minute.

I don't know why I buy into these unspoken opinions. I don't know why I cannot hang that proverbial sign on the rhetorical door and force family members to fend for themselves for a few short hours every day.

One thing I don't buy into, though, is the theory that I must not take my writing seriously. I do. I've wanted to be a writer since grade school. I've accomplished some things with my writing, more now than ever. However, I think I take my family seriously too. What I need to do is find a way to help them understand the difference between needing me to do things for them and simply wanting me to do those things.

And, I suppose, a little shot of writing-self-esteem and a suppression of that conflict-guilt would go a long way toward finding daily time to write. After all, even Cinderella found time to make that dress and go to the ball. Granted, she had a bunch of singing mice to help, but as I look around my office at the guinea pig enclosure behind me (housing little Murray, who keeps me company up here), I somehow don't see him singing and cooking up a nice dinner for me so I can spend my time writing instead.

And now, if you'll excuse me, I have to put the laundry into the dryer and run to the store. We're out of milk. Again.   ❖

Blood, Sweat and Tears

I'm not quite fifty years old and my body—coincidentally, the only one I own—is rebelling against me. Some of it is my own fault, but the way my various parts work together to work against me has been a little daunting in recent years. I've grouped all my annoying ailments into three categories: blood, sweat and tears.

BLOOD

At age forty-eight I was diagnosed with Type 2 diabetes. The only good thing I can say about diabetes is that it's an excuse to eat every three hours, even if it is stuff like cole slaw and scrambled eggs all the time. I can hear you now: "Wow, this is going to be hilarious because diabetes is so damn funny!" I agree: What's funnier than Wilford Brimley peddling ways to have miniature torture devices delivered straight to your door? Gotta love the Brim-man.

Although I have no empirical evidence to back this up, I suspect there is a vast pop-culture hierarchy within the diabetic community that measures a person's inherent worth by the brand of his testing meter and the size of his lancing device. I've been a diagnosed diabetic for about five months and I already own four glucose-testing meters. I'm thinking of starting a collection the way some people collect Hummel figurines or Star Wars action figures. Maybe I'll get a nice oak curio cabinet to display them all. This disease and all these free meters are bringing out the gadget-geek in me. The way free meters show up at my door, it's like Christmas every day at our house—minus the cookies. If I make it look like any more fun, my husband will start wantonly wolfing down ice cream sundaes and birthday cake just so he can get free meters in the mail too.

So, with the eagerness you'd expect from someone who's just learned she gets to poke herself in the finger with a needle-sharp object half a dozen times a day for the rest of her life, I began my journey into the wonderful world of deliberately bleeding like a stuck pig. The first time I used the lancet* to poke a small hole in my fingertip in order to withdraw my own lifeblood, I had

*Note: "Lancet" is just not a happy word. It makes me think of medieval jousting. And frankly, after using one for the past few months, that initial assessment ain't too far off.

to change it to its deepest setting to see enough blood to use on the test strip. *Good grief, do I have skin made of tree bark or what?*

The testing itself isn't all that bad, but I constantly fight off the urge to test family members at indiscriminate moments throughout the day, preferably when they're not looking:

"Grace, hold still—and look over there while I just . . . What? Oh, nothing. Wait, come back!"

"Oh, Jeremy, how terrible that you just cut yourself with a serrated kitchen knife! That reminds me: Are you using that blood for anything special? Why? Well, because I want to—No, it's not *that* crazy!"

Now nobody will get within twenty-five feet of me without wearing battle armor or chain mail. And the guinea pig is looking a little too nervous these days.

SWEAT

I've gained weight in my middle age. If the adage is true that muscle weighs more than fat, this certainly wouldn't explain the scale, though. Except that I can't make it up the front steps without a spotter, some semaphore flags, and an oxygen tank.

Calling my life sedentary is like calling water wet. I work from home in my own office upstairs, and it was once a kitchen when the house was two apartments. The up side to this arrangement (besides commuting in my jammies) is that my office has cupboards for storing office supplies, a countertop for small book racks and my editor's desk, a smooth linoleum floor for zipping the wheeled office chair around, and a sink—which is actually the bad part too. The sink gave me the brilliant idea to put a small coffeemaker and a dorm fridge on the countertop so I can brew coffee up here and then store the creamer and cans of diet soda (and veggies for Murray, the guinea pig—certainly not for *me*) in the fridge. Add to the room an ethernet jack, a cable television outlet, a cheap DVD player, two printers, two monitors, a phone, an iPod dock, two file cabinets, and an electric stapler, and I never need to get out of my chair or leave the room. (Okay, maybe the stapler isn't all that necessary.) Some weeks I don't move a muscle from Monday through Thursday. Give me a catheter and a sofabed and you won't see me till next February.

All this physical inactivity (which creates a heightened sense of self-awareness if I attune my soul to it— although that could just be the second cup of coffee talking) has led to an advanced case of middle-aged spread. Once my three main body measurements were exactly the same, I knew it was time to get off my derriere. Time to turn that Health Rider back into a piece of finely crafted exercise equipment. *But,* I thought, *where will I put the clothing that's been hanging on the handlebars since 1999? I don't want to drag all those hangers all the way downstairs to my bedroom closet. That would tire me out.* . . .

Soon I'll have to take exercising seriously, if only to stop getting winded while walking the twenty-five feet from the driveway to the front door. I've heard exercising isn't successful without long-term goals.

TEARS

A few years ago I gave up reading anything for more than twenty minutes because my eyes began to sting just as I was getting to the good parts. The work I did in front of a computer screen during the day was killing my sedentary, silent, solitary social life at night. Until my eye doctor saved the day by suggesting I might have ocular rosacea and chronic dry eye.

At first this diagnosis made no sense, because my eyes gush tears with one sip of carbonated soda or with one small sneeze or sudden movement. She explained that this is precisely what dry-eye sufferers endure: The eyes emit tears at all the wrong times (like, in the middle of Will Ferrell movies or in front of your teenager's friends at the mall), and they don't lubricate the eyeball properly—or something like that. I missed half of what she said because her office is in the mall and my teenager was meeting her friends in the Forever 21 store in five minutes and I'd begun to blink back tears in anticipation.

So now I have over-the-counter-and-through-the-woods drops for my eyes, antibacterial wipes for my eyelids, antibiotics measured in fractions of an ounce for forty bucks after the copay, and recurrent followup appointments (but only on days ending in "y" during months with an "r"). It's a lot of work just so I can stare at the computer screen a little longer without weeping, or just so I can read another chapter of the latest Outlander novel before nodding off in the comfy chair at night. I wonder if all that work counts as exercise.

The logical conclusion of all this annoying bodily upheaval is that we're mortal—and, on most days, me more than anyone else. As I rapidly approach the start of my second century on the planet, I have this ugly feeling in the pit of my pathetically ample stomach that it's not going to get any better from this point on. Yet another reason for the tears, methinks.   ♣

Still More Random Things I Notice

List #3: Remember When . . .

- . . . you could order a cup of coffee by saying "coffee" without having to play 20 Questions with a barista born thirty years after the demise of the coffee pot?
- . . . the only butt cracks you saw in public belonged to refrigerator repairmen and weren't walking the halls of the local high school going to history class? Or teaching it?
- . . . family pets had pet names like Fluffy and Rover and Spot and Whiskers, instead of human names like Bob and Fred and Chloe?
- . . . babies had human names like Bob and Fred and Chloe, instead of names of inanimate or unknown objects, like Apple and Dweezil and Snake?

• . . . you could buy big roomy clothes like bathrobes that were marked "One size fits all"? I recently bought a bathrobe with this on the label: **"One size fits most."** Most? What happened? Did some porky chick buy the robe when the label read "One size fits all," and when she discovered she couldn't tie the belt, did she sue them for false advertising? Then again, she has a point. How do they know their robes fit absolutely everybody? Doesn't that seem like a bad way to label a piece of clothing, statistically speaking? If it was a woman's robe, it'd have to fit over three billion people for their label to be accurate.

• . . . the one television your family owned got twelve channels . . . on a knob . . . *on* the television . . . and the "remote control" was you?   ♣

Gravity

(an old poem now dedicated to Wayne)

I sat under the apple tree,
Just thinking of my love.
He's tall and blond and dashing too,
Sent down from heav'n above.

I looked up at the deep blue sky
And watched the swallows rise.
The blue grew deeper endlessly
Just like my lover's eyes.

The golden rays of summer's sun
Shone on me all the while.
It gave a tingling warmth to all
Just like my lover's smile.

An apple drops down from the tree;
My head splits it in half.
I hear a chuckle from above,
Just like my lover's laugh!

Beware of Geeks Bearing Gifts

My cherished husband, Wayne, is currently tweaking a home computer server he built from spare parts and stuff he bought cheap on eBay. This means my living room decor goes from "country/traditional" to "computerpartscablesandwireseverywheresowatchwhereyoustep."

What this meant for me was not only losing my living room to electronic gadgetry but also a lot of "Can you hear me now?"-type problem-solving. Trial and error is a wonderful thing, but once it takes over the living room, no real work gets done. Books don't get read in the comfy wing chair. Manuscripts don't get edited on the couch. Bad reality television doesn't get watched from the recliner. Mass hysteria soon follows.

Instead, freakishly gargantuan CPUs (on wheels,

no less—the big kind that come on office chairs) with cooling fans the size of New Jersey move noisily around the room, taking with them enough CAT5 cable for a tech school training class on a bad day. Each slot that now houses its own huge hard drive (bought on sale somewhere with rebates and coupons) hums happily and adds its own din to the whirr and buzz of the fan, and if I need white noise, I know where to turn.

What I really need, though, is a quiet place to work. And right now, the living room—with this computer/coffee table and the massive seventeen-inch CRT monitor tethered to it—is not the place. White noise is one thing, but once you have to turn up the television to earsplitting ranges, risking the hearing of all the neighborhood dogs, well, then, the battle is lost.

Sometimes I'm grateful for the home office I maintain here . . . upstairs.   ♣

Fishing for Compliments

My elder daughter and I went on our first fishing trip this past Saturday. We bought twelve-dollar fishing rods at Walmart, and the necessary gear, including nightcrawlers. Who knew you could buy live bait at Walmart? (Well, *you* might have, but I certainly didn't. Although, thinking about it later, it made perfect sense.)

We decided to try Brady's Run, a few short miles away, and got there around one P.M. Within about fifteen to twenty seconds of plunking her line into the water, Grace realized a small sunfish had decided to hop on for the ride. We threw the little guy back, but he served to encourage us in our endeavor. Two and a half hours later we came home with three fish, the largest of which was about ten inches long.

Grace cleaned them all herself, and then cooked them in olive oil and garlic along with some lemon juice. Scales and bones aside (and sadly, they weren't aside—they were still attached to the fish), the actual meat itself was marvelous—all twenty-seven molecules of it.

We learned a few lessons that we're going to use on our next camping trip:

1. Scale the fish. *Scale it.* I don't care how annoying and dull and difficult it is, **scale it, stupid.**

2. Throw even the semi-little ones back. They're really not going to be worth the effort of cleaning them, especially if you're not going to **scale them, you idiot.**

3. If you fish with a second person, don't stand too close to each other while casting your lines into the water. You only have two eyes, remember? And lips don't like to have holes in them. At least mine don't.

4. Some fish are stupid enough to meander around in the water a foot from shore. Even ten-inch fish. Sometimes. So, be ready to just walk to the edge and drop your line down into the water and yank it back out with a fish attached. It can happen to you.

5. If you bring a five-gallon plastic bucket to put the fish in, don't forget to bring a lid. One that stays on. Who knew local fish were also *flying* fish? If you have no lid, don't put the bucket too close to the water. You've been warned.

6. If you are using nightcrawlers in dirt, and if you are handling your own fish to take them off the hook, bring wet wipes. Trust me on this one. Especially if you also packed a lunch and haven't eaten it yet.

Despite the misadventures of the day, we're really psyched to go fishing at Laurel Hill Campground in less than two weeks! Trout dinner over an open fire, here we come! As long as we remember to *scale them, stupid!*   ♣

A Blaze of Glory

My everlasting beloved works at the local nuclear power plant. (Think Homer Simpson minus the doughnuts. No, wait, keep the doughnuts.) You probably have a local grocery store or a local basketball team. And we have a local nuclear power plant. Doesn't everybody?

Tonight at dinner Wayne's telling me a my-day-at-work story and I'm listening while crunching my salad.

"So then Blaze says . . ."

"Wait, who?"

"Blaze."

"The guy's nickname is Blaze?"

"No, that's his name."

I have to think about this for a while. Crunch. Crunch. Crunch.

"His first name?"

"Yup."

Crunchety crunch crunch. I don't ask what his last name is.

Despite the fact that the story is not going this way, my mind is wandering elsewhere. I am sitting here in awe of parents brave enough to name their baby boy Blaze when they could have named him Justin or Joshua or Sean or something equally conformist. What an attitude this kid must have had during his school years! What cheers he must have heard at graduation when his name was called!

Then again, do you really want a guy named Blaze working at your local nuke plant?

Three months later, though, I got the rest of the story (no thanks to Paul Harvey). You know, the part I cared about—that weird name.

Naturally, while having a conversation (especially one with an engineer and not a fellow writer), no one's spelling out what they're saying letter by letter (unless there are small children around and you're trying to talk about **s-e-x**).

Imagine my embarrassment to find out that our nuke plant worker, Blaze, had parents who in actuality named him **Blasé.**

So it is a normal name after all, if a bit on the exotic side. But I bet he still got beat up on the playground. ✤

Even More Random Things I Notice

List #4: Really Arbitrary Observations

• Power outages at home are fun—for about fifteen minutes. Then the teenagers figure out that the Internet is down, the cable TV isn't working, and it's difficult to read celebrity magazines by candlelight without setting something on fire.

• All haircuts are great for the first few weeks, but one day the haircut goes nuts and doesn't remember where any of your hairs should go and cowlicks show up unbidden.

• Some days I have so little intestinal fortitude that the only staring contest I can win is with the goldfish, and even then it's a close call because he doesn't have eyelids.

• Parents gush with pride over their children's tiniest accomplishments because they remember when the most difficult thing their kids did was refrain from pooping in their pants, and they're just grateful the kids have moved beyond doing that sort of thing in public.

• I have to feel adventurous before I'll clean the top of the refrigerator. Going up there is akin to exploring the lunar surface. Last time I cleaned up there, I found some moon rocks and a U.S. flag next to the Cheerios box.   ❧

Sunny Side Down

Have you ever awakened too early—accidentally? You know, you wake up while it's still half-dark outside, then realize you're way too awake to go back to sleep, so you get up anyway?

Yeah, me neither.

Well, actually, I did that this past week. Twice. Once, I could forgive. But the second time was just downright rude. I could have slept an extra hour or more but my body was saying it needed to visit a bathroom, and then my brain said, "While we're up, why don't we just check our e-mail real quick?"

Then my body said, "This couch is so comfortable. Why don't we just stay here and put on the news and see if anything big happened overnight?"

Which, of course, nothing did.

By now it was eight o'clock, so I said to myself, "Might as well just stay up now. I'll never get back to sleep at this point."

I could have smacked myself for that last thought (well, and the other ones before that too), but I never win when I argue with myself so I let it slide this once and stayed up.

Then it happened again a few days later. Got up at seven-thirty when I could have slept in for another hour and gotten a full eight hours' sleep. But no, I checked e-mail, fed the guinea pigs, and generally putzed around before I had to shower and get ready to take my daughter out for a few errands.

I just hope it doesn't turn into a habit. If I suddenly became a morning person, I think I'd have to kill myself. But I wouldn't do it till at least noon.   ❖

You're Positively Glowing!

Did you ever eat lunch at a nuke plant?

Yeah, me neither—until this week. It wasn't what I expected—partly because I'm not allowed very far inside the perimeter and stayed in the public areas near the outer edge of the plant. But I did get to drive by all the cooling towers. Cooling towers are those round concave buildings that just scream "China Syndrome!" and "Silkwood!" and "Three Mile Island!" I drove through the tiny town of Shippingport, which boasts these five cooling towers as the main part of its skyline (a term I use loosely in reference to Shippingport).

I've heard a rumor that the town's residents, in exchange for rearing their children in the shadow of a nuclear power plant, get free cable TV. You know, something worthwhile and comparable to their woes. Something the families with six kids (and twelve heads) can really make use of.

But I digress. Nobody I saw while meeting my husband for a quick lunch had a second head. Wayne did look suspiciously like an overgrown Mickey Mouse, but that was because he was wearing a white hardhat with gray sound-muffling earphones perched on the sides of the hat. Before then, I'd never pictured Mickey Mouse as six-foot-four, blond, mustachioed, and walking pigeon-toed in a denim work shirt.

Or eating a foot-long pastrami sandwich from Subway. But, amazingly, there he was. Not glowing, either, which was a relief. Oh, and wearing forty thousand I.D. badges and cards and keys and lanyards around his neck—all of which probably weighed as much as a small Toyota. Bling for the engineering homeboys.

I kept expecting to hear a siren go off and then to watch everyone hit the deck. You know, like in every movie with a nuke plant in it. Or perhaps I'd see a security guard with a semiautomatic weapon (yes, before you ask, they do, but don't ask) running up to me and asking to see my forty thousand I.D. badges and lanyards, which of course I don't have.

I got out of there unscathed, and the nuke plant continues to make clean, efficient electricity for everyone—including the two-headed residents of Shippingport.   ❖

Another Foot in the Grave

True story: My younger daughter and I were eating pizza and watching the movie *That Thing You Do!* on TV. We were watching my favorite scene—where Liv Tyler's character, Faye, is mailing a letter while wearing a radio earplug, and the Wonders' new song comes on the radio for the first time. She licks a stamp and then dumps the letter in the mailbox and goes screaming down the street in ecstasy.

Daughter, to me: "Mom, in that scene she's licking the postage stamp before she puts it on the letter. Why is she doing that? Wouldn't you just stick it on the envelope?"

I just about fell over. Surely within my daughter's memory and lifetime there have been postage stamps you had to lick, right? Surely she was kidding and she did remember you once had to lick postage stamps? No, she hadn't a clue that there was a time when you couldn't just peel a stamp off its backing and stick it to the envelope.

Meanwhile, I rarely go through a batch of stamps where I don't fleetingly think, "I'm so glad I don't have to lick all these stamps like I used to have to do. They always tasted like old cough medicine."

In other words, something that still seems new to me (peelable stamps) seems like it's always been that way to my daughter, who is already taller than I am and is learning to drive.

Good grief, another foot in the grave. By my count, that's about six or seven feet so far, though, so, really, I should be glad to be here at all.

I need to remind myself never to show her a rotary phone. Or a percolator.   ❖

Hook, Line and Sinker

When I was a teen, my paternal grandmother, Fannie Mae Hockenberry Au, patiently taught me how to crochet. She had tried to teach my mother this skill in years past, but apparently you must carry an actual Hockenberry gene because my mother never quite got the knack if it. As for my own training, after some figurative and literal hand-holding by my eternally patient grandmother, I picked up the basics of crocheting. For a long while the stitches were uneven and ugly, and doing anything but straight lines back and forth was an impossibility. And the term "straight lines" was a compliment my work didn't deserve.

But over the years since those early lessons I've done several projects that were zigzag, or round, or had different patterns. And I've found that crocheting fulfills a basic desire to create something—something from (almost) nothing. There's a sense of satisfaction in completing a project. I'm at the stage now where I hurry to complete one crocheting project just so I can move on to another. There has to be a disorder named after that, doesn't there? Arts and Crafts A.D.D.?

However, now I have leftover skeins of yarn from each project. (I always buy too much yarn for a project. There's nothing worse than getting toward the end of a project and only then finding out your afghan is now going to be the size of a large dish towel because of your poor planning.) I may feel brave enough someday to make an afghan out of all those wacky mismatched leftover skeins. It would still be warm and the stitches would still be even. But where on God's good earth could I put it? It'd be an eyesore. A nice, comfy eyesore, but still, an eyesore.

So, if you know me personally and one day you get an afghan of, well, unusual color schemes, for lack of a better term, think of it as recycling. I'm just trying to be eco-friendly.

During my decades of crocheting—the thousands of hours spent crippling my own fingers with an aluminum hook—I've amassed a small amount of needlecraft wisdom I feel compelled to pass along to the neophytes within my readership. So, jot this stuff down; you might need it someday. (Wait, you don't need to jot it down—you bought this book and here it all is. And if you're borrowing a friend's copy, shame on you! Stop reading now and go buy your own copy, you skinflint.)

• My experience with mismatched skein ends has taught me that this is how the granny square was invented. Which, come to think of it, gives me an idea.

• If you are a slow crocheter, you should double-check to be sure ponchos will still be in style before you crochet twenty of them for your nieces (and nephews). The same goes for berets. And neckties. And sweater vests. Take a walk through your local thrift store if you don't believe me.

• If you don't have air conditioning, remember to crochet tiny, lacy items in July and big, hefty afghans in December. Nothing sucks worse than having a mammoth ripple afghan draped across your lap when it's hot enough to melt the linoleum in your kitchen and humid enough to moisten Uncle Earl's chapped lips.

• Friends don't let friends drink and crochet.   ♣

Word Brain Versus Math Brain

We've all heard the expression "Oil and water don't mix." And yet, my husband, Wayne, and I are so different in so many ways that I wonder if I ought to check his shirt label to see if he's a different genus or subspecies from me. Because honestly, most of the time I don't get how his brain works. To boil it down: I'm a writer and he's an electrical engineer. That's fairly far apart along the spectrum of vocational light.

The simplest way to express our rudimentary difference is that I'm a word brain and he's a math brain. I think in logical **word** pictures (okay, not always *logical*), and he thinks in logical **number** pictures, mechanical pictures. I love books and papers, and he loves gadgets and objects and things. I think; he does. I'll theorize; he'll simonize.

We're both collectors—but not very official ones. So, while I stack neverending book purchases on already sagging bookcases and keep reams of 96-bright laserjet-compatible paper in my office cabinets, Wayne stuffs rolls of ethernet cable, blue plastic electrical outlet boxes, and roofing nails into large plastic totes. I hoard red pens and paper clips; he hoards ratchet sets and blank rewritable CDs.

There are a few of his "math brain" things lying around the house that perplex me, though—in ways that can't be easily explained by the word brain/math brain dichotomy. The first is a small cardboard box that reads "Professional Soldering Station." Don't misunderstand me: I get why a guy wants—and even needs—a soldering station. I'm cool with the whole "I need to burn stuff but not get arrested or sent to a psych evaluation for it" mentality.

What puzzles me is the obvious question raised by the wording on the box of the Professional Soldering Station: Is there such a thing as an *Amateur* Soldering Station? And, given the nature and temperature of soldering, in addition to its close proximity to one's fingers, would anyone rush out to buy one? Besides Wayne, that is, who placed as first runnerup in the local Mr. Clearance Rack contest three years straight?

The second item of confusion is really two items. He currently owns two shop-vacs: one that really sucks (which means it works), and one that really, *really* sucks (which means it doesn't work). That second one seems redundant, if nothing else.

The third item that baffles me is really about twenty items, and they're all currently residing in Wayne's office. They're all the computer cases and CPUs from every computer each of us has owned since the mid-nineties. (For you word brains out there, that's over fifteen years ago—last century, last millennium. Get a calculator. I already double-checked the math on this one.) I'm not sure what his plans are, but I'm guessing one of two things: Either he's going to open a technology museum in the back of our house, or he's planning to take over the world with his own private bank of computer servers able to run multiple heavy-duty software applications and hack into government mainframes the world over.

All that intrigue sounds mildly fascinating, as long as I conveniently forget that most of those old computers are missing power supplies, hard drives or motherboards and the software loaded onto the remaining servers is stuff like free online poker games and shareware programs that change photos of people you don't like and stretch them into funny shapes. But, hey, I could do that stretchy thing back in the 1970s with a hunk of Silly Putty and a newspaper.

So, while Wayne is busy taking over the world one royal flush at a time, I'll be recataloguing my books, promising myself to get rid of some of them, and then tossing out Wayne's old college textbooks instead.

In the perpetual war of the word brain versus the math brain, the word brain wins another battle—but perhaps not the war. There is still that shop-vac to contend with.   ♣

"I Need You to Trust Me on This"

I'm trying to catch up to everyone else in the world who's been watching *24*. God bless Netflix for allowing me to catch up on TV series. (First *Lost*, now this.) I just finished Season 3 today. Watching the episodes back to back to back to back, I'm noticing patterns—and I'm guessing the patterns hold throughout the rest of the series' history. Here's my list so far:

• Always have a mole inside CTU. It makes for extra excitement just when things are going right everywhere else.

• Have Jack Bauer shoot someone under iffy circumstances at least twice per season. More, if you can get away with it. And you can *always* get away with it.

• Everybody has to talk in a really raspy voice and sound breathless at all times.

- Have Jack go renegade every other episode, so that people back at CTU can pair off in groups of "helping Jack" versus "totally out of the loop with Jack."

- Each actor in the series gets fifteen minutes of total self-righteous overacting every season (cue raspy breathless voices here). It's in their contracts.

- Viruses and bombs get released/detonated but then are revealed as false alarms, so that they can be released/detonated again—at least three times in that single twenty-four-hour day.

- Apparently technology has invented a cell phone model that never needs its battery recharged, and CTU bought them all.

- No one ever eats or goes to the bathroom during the entire twenty-four-hour period. And with all that takeout coffee they drink, that's quite a feat. Evidently they all wear Depends or something. I still want to see an episode with Jack Bauer careening that SUV through a Jack-in-the-Box drive-thru and ordering some large fries and a root beer.

- People at CTU who get wounded in the early part of the day (shot, stabbed, preferably both) can get by with very small amounts of medical attention before going straight back to work for another eighteen-plus hours. They're then given another fifteen minutes of self-righteous overacting (with raspy breathless voices) to compensate for the really bad day they're having.

- *"Brrrrrr-dee-dee-doop!"* Those phones in CTU are really going to drive me crazy by the time I work my way up to Season 35.

- Why doesn't anyone ever say to Jack, "Have a nice day"?

- Someone at CTU will be charged with treason at least once per season—and then turn out to be the most patriotic person on the show.

- This is supposed to be the most high-tech place on the planet, but yet, whenever it's convenient, even low-level employees can find a way to do something untraceable or go offline and off-grid and not get caught. Oh, and they're always the ones who work right in the middle of the main floor where everyone can see them. Doesn't this place have better security cameras? Two words, people: *browser history.*

- Why doesn't that place have proper lighting, even in the middle of the day? It's like watching a crime scene workover from *CSI* with all that cool high-tech mood lighting everywhere. Three words, people: *hundred-watt bulbs!*

C'mon, CTU! I shouldn't have to keep telling you people this stuff. Aren't you supposed to be the smartest people on Earth? Or is that only on some *other* day we never get to see? ❖

Definition of a Bad Day

I'm checking all the international dateline stuff all over the world, just to make sure yesterday is officially over . . . *everywhere.*

Here's the quick-and-dirty of what went down yesterday that made it so, uh, memorable:

• **Late morning to mid-afternoon:** My elder son and I stand in the scorching heat in gravel parking lots looking at used cars. The noon news has declared this an official "ozone action day." I have no idea what this means. I want to do as little action as possible, and I'm sure the ozone agrees with me.

• **Mid-afternoon:** Son signs 2.7 million pieces of paper and makes several phone calls to the insurance company to set up proper paperwork to drive a 1990 Buick Century off the lot. One owner. Primo condition.

Nicer than any car I've ever owned. Which is sad. We are all pleased, and I secretly hope to get the gecko's autograph.

• **Early evening:** Hubby comes home from work, hobbling on his bad knee. He has had to climb ladders this week, his first week back after being on crutches for aforementioned bad knee. I feed him and son hamburgers and hot dogs (which I grill outside on the sidewalk to save money on propane), and waffle fries. (Despite the name "waffle fries," I refrain from putting syrup on the table. Evidently a misnomer.) We all have a special bonding time talking about first cars and the excitement of new apartments and new lives. I sniffle. Son rolls his eyes.

• **7:30 P.M.:** Son packs up car and heads off so that he can work in the morning and start moving into new apartment.

• **7:45 P.M.:** Son calls on cell phone from three miles down the street to say the battery light has come on. Hubby tells him to turn around and come back.

• **8:00 to 8:30 P.M.:** Local auto parts store assures them alternator is good, so it must be the four-year-old battery. Son buys new battery. Naturally, they don't have any of the low-cost batteries in stock, only the "Titanium" ones.

• **8:30 P.M.:** The three-block trip back to the house to pick up his stuff reveals that the battery light is still on. Hubby determines with one of his electrical-engineer-magical-gadgets that it is indeed the alternator causing the problems. His knee is screaming a third chorus of

"Battle Hymn of the Republic" in some Scandinavian language, so he bows out of changing alternator in the dark. I sniffle. Son rolls his eyes.

- **8:45 P.M.:** Son gives up on getting back to his place for the night, and makes twenty-seven necessary phone calls to rearrange his schedule.

- **10:00 P.M.:** Depressed, son decides to make a bag of microwave popcorn in our new microwave, not noticing the button marked "Popcorn" and instead setting it for four minutes on high . . . and goes upstairs to do something while waiting. Waiting? Apparently four minutes is an eternity to his generation.

- **10:03:45 P.M.:** I naively say to no one in particular, "Is something burning?" and realize I still hear the microwave humming in the kitchen, although the popping sound has long since stopped.

- **10:04 P.M.:** The inside of the microwave now has a brownish yellow film permanently burned onto its inside walls, and the smell of burnt popcorn permeates the neighboring counties.

- **11:00 P.M.:** I am weary and cranky and I feel like a bad mother. So I do the only natural thing: I go to bed early and hide.

- **9:00 A.M.:** I wake up early to call the local mechanic to ask about taking an alternator we buy elsewhere and quick-changing it for us on the fly. He agrees. I make a mental note to add him to our Christmas card list.

- **9:01 A.M.:** I go upstairs to alert son. Well, okay, to wake him out of a dead sleep. Clearly, "alert" is a relative term. Son sniffles. I roll my eyes.

• **9:02 A.M.:** I decide to slip into my office across the hall and check mail and get back to the real world . . . a place I've forgotten over the past two days. I see a note near my computer from one of the other kids: "Mom, last night I threw up because of the burnt popcorn smell. It was around 4 A.M. and I didn't want to wake you or Chris up. I don't know the first thing about cleaning up throw-up, so I left it by the side of my bed."

Is it tomorrow yet?

It's now noon, and son left again this morning, after mechanic did a flawless quick-change of old dirty alternator to new shiny alternator for very little money. Son left around eleven o'clock, so I should be hearing from him soon at the other end of his trip.

I just hope it's not a call about the engine light. Because I'm officially declaring yesterday over.

Final update: Eventually, son made it back home with no more car problems. Nothing burned or exploded. No one threw up. The world as we know it didn't end.

I'm taking a nap. Wake me in September.   ♣

Dead Lines

(a poem written for no reason)

The clock is ticking off the hours,
One thought dies, another cowers.
The page is filled with penned red lines:
One word stinks, the other shines.

My mind's devoid of all its powers,
Ideas ripen—then each sours.
My scattered thoughts make no headlines;
In fact, they mostly just shred lines.

Editors think, "Let's disavow hers,
Since every line can't rhyme with 'flowers'!"
Now I'll end up in those bread lines
Unless I make a few deadlines.

* * * * *